GALLOWAY COUNTY PUBLIC LIBRARY
710 Main Street
MURRAY, KY 42071

WITHDRAWN

Physical Characteristics
of the Fila Brasileiro
(from the FCI breed standard)

Body: Strong, broad and deep, covered by thick and loose skin.

Skin: A very important characteristic of the breed is the loose skin. Thick and most prominent at the neck where it forms accentuated dewlaps.

Tail: Very wide at the root, medium set, reaching to the level of the hocks, tapering rapidly at its end.

Height: At the withers: males 65—75 cms (25.5—29.5 in); females 60–70 cms (23.5–27.5 in).

Weight: Males minimum of 50 kgs (110 lb); females minimum of 40 kg (88 lb).

Forelegs: Must be parallel, straight to the pasterns and with powerful bones.

Feet: Formed by strong and well arched toes, which are not close together. The correct position of the feet is pointing to the front.

D1297126

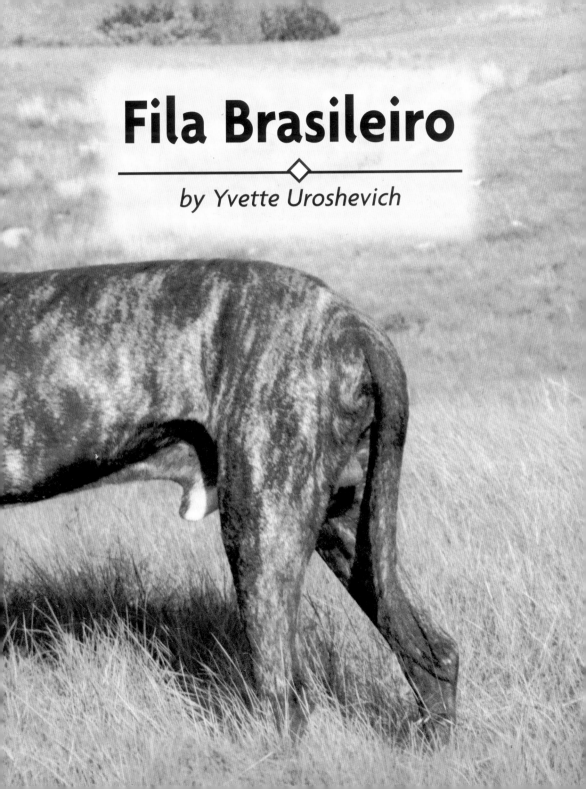

Fila Brasileiro

by Yvette Uroshevich

Contents

Training Your Fila Brasileiro 88

By Charlotte Schwartz
Be informed about the importance of training your Fila Brasileiro from the basics of housebreaking and understanding the development of a young dog to executing obedience commands (sit, stay, down, etc.).

Health Care of Your Fila Brasileiro 116

Discover how to select a qualified vet and care for your dog at all stages of life. Topics include vaccinations, skin problems, dealing with external and internal parasites and common medical and behavioral conditions.

Showing Your Fila Brasileiro 114

Enter the dog show world and find out how dog shows work and how to make a champion. Go beyond the conformation ring to obedience trials and agility trials, etc.

Behavior of Your Fila Brasileiro 148

Learn to recognize and handle behavioral problems that may arise with your Fila Brasileiro. Topics discussed include separation anxiety, aggression, barking, chewing, digging, begging, jumping up, etc.

Photographs by:
Mike Bancroft/Eshabeta Kennels, Norvia Behling,
Dawna Berg/Eshabeta Kennels, T. J. Calhoun, Carolina Biological Supply,
Doskocil, Isabelle Français, James Hayden-Yoav, James R. Hayden, RBP,
Clelia Kruel/Camping Kennels, Dwight R. Kuhn, Dr. Dennis Kunkel,
Mikki Pet Products, Phototake, Jean Claude Revy, Alice Roche,
Dr. Andrew Spielman, Judy Theriot, Yvette Uroshevich, Alice van Kempen
and C. James Webb.

The owner wishes to thank the owners of the dogs featured in this book, including
Camping Kennel, Eshabeta Kennels, Ali Geese, Mark and Kathy Koch,
Jason Ogresovich, Francis Osinski, Judy Theriot, Susan C. Williams,
Yvette Uroshevich and Bonnie and Lee Young.

Illustrations by Renée Low

KENNEL CLUB BOOKS: FILA BRASILEIRO
ISBN: 1-59378-219-5

Copyright © 1999 • Revised American Edition: Copyright © 2003
Kennel Club Books, Inc., 308 Main Street, Allenhurst, NJ 07711 USA
Cover Design Patented: US 6,435,559 B2 • Printed in South Korea

All rights reserved. No part of this book may be reproduced in any form, by photostat, scanner, microfilm, xerography or any other means, or incorporated into any information retrieval system, electronic or mechanical, without the written permission of the copyright owner.

The Fila Brasileiro is a big dog, afraid of nothing and aloof to strangers. He is extremely loyal to his masters and is used extensively in Brazil as a working dog on farms and ranches.

HISTORY OF THE
FILA BRASILEIRO

THE GENESIS OF THE BREED IN ITS HOMELAND

The Fila Brasileiro is not a man-made breed, but one that developed naturally because of Brazil's early colonists' need for a strong, hardy working dog. These first Filas can be seen in historical documents as early as 1671. The exact roots of these early Filas are not known. However, most people agree that the Fila Brasileiro is a combination of three basic breeds—ancient bulldogs, Mastiffs and Bloodhounds. It is also thought by some that the Fila Terceirense may have played a part in the development of the Fila Brasileiro.

•   One of the breeds that contributed to the Fila Brasileiro was the Engelsen Doggen. These ancient bulldogs were often used for hunting and fighting. They were brought to Brazil during the Dutch invasion around 1630. From the Engelsen Doggen, the Fila Brasileiro inherited his aggressive temperament, stubbornness and tenacity. Some of the physical traits these ancient bulldogs share with the modern Fila Brasileiro are the "rose ear," the colors of the coat and a higher croup than the withers, which is one of the identifying traits of the Fila Brasileiro.

The influence of the English Mastiff is clearly visible in the Fila Brasileiro. From these large, ferocious dogs the Fila acquired his size and substance. These ancient Mastiffs, often used in battle and hunting sports, also passed the large, heavy head, the short neck and the curved croup on to the Fila Brasileiro. The Mastiff and Fila Brasileiro share the same basic coat colors and the black mask as well.

Bloodhounds were imported to Brazil in the early 1800s because of their reputation as excellent trackers. The Bloodhound passed his scenting ability on to the Fila Brasileiro. An abundance of loose skin, pendulous lips and hanging flews and dewlaps, obvious characteristics of the Bloodhound, can also be seen in the Fila. Anyone who owns a Fila Brasileiro can tell you that the vocalizations of the Bloodhound are present in the Fila of today. Many Fila owners claim that their dogs have a language all their own!

The English Mastiff contributed his bulk, giant head and substance to the Fila. Both breeds also share the same basic coat colors.

Another theory speculates that a fourth breed had a paw in the development of the Fila Brasileiro. This is the Fila Terceirense, a herding dog brought by Portuguese colonists from the Azores Islands. It would explain the cattle-herding ability of the Fila Brasileiro and may explain another trait sometimes seen in Filas, in which the tail has a twist that makes it change directions to the side. This physical characteristic is the reason the Fila is sometimes called "crooked tail" or "broken tail" in his homeland of Brazil.

The Great Dane cannot claim much credit for the great Fila, although some were introduced into Fila lines well into the breed's development.

Around 1930, Great Danes were becoming very popular in Brazil. Although the Fila was well established as a breed by this time, some breeders tried to intro-duce Great Dane blood into the Fila Brasileiro. These crossings were numerically insignificant and did nothing to improve the breed. It was found at this time that trying to add new breeds to the Fila Brasileiro could only harm, and not improve, the balanced temperament of the Fila.

In 1968, Dr. Erwin Rathsam, along with Dr. Paulo Santos Cruz and Dr. João Ebner, wrote the first official standard for the breed. Until this time, the Fila Brasileiro was viewed solely as a working breed. The first Filas were shown in Brazil at this time and judged by the new standard. Not all Filas went into the show ring; many continued in their roles as working dogs. These working dogs did not even have pedigrees. They

The Bloodhound was used to improve the scenting ability of the Fila, as the Bloodhound's nose is his most legendary trait. Additionally, the Bloodhound contributed his loose skin, lips, flews and dewlaps.

were bred solely for their working abilities.

The Fédération Cynologique Internationale (FCI) officially recognized the Fila Brasileiro breed in 1968. The standard was introduced around Europe, including England, Holland and Italy. The standard remained unchanged for almost a decade. Then, in 1976, the first symposium on the Fila Brasileiro was held in Brazil. The standard was revised at this time. The Fila Brasileiro continued to grow in popularity until 1982, when it became the most popular breed in Brazil with 8,087 puppies officially registered (according to the Brazilian Confederation Kennel Club).

In 1983, a great National Congress was held in Rio de Janeiro. The purpose was to determine breeding practices for the Fila Brasileiro and to discuss revisions to the breed standard. A more detailed standard was the result of this meeting. The new standard, which became official on January 1, 1994, is still used today.

ORIGINAL PURPOSE OF THE BREED

The Fila Brasileiro is a breed that met the needs of the people of Brazil. These early colonists needed a hard-working dog that could perform many tasks. They needed a guard dog, a herding dog, a hunter and a loyal compan-

CALLOWAY COUNTY PUBLIC LIBRARY
710 Main Street
MURRAY KY 42071

ion. All of these traits, and many more, are found in the Fila Brasileiro.

The Colonial period in Brazil was a time of grand sugar plantations. Many workers were needed to keep these plantations going, so African slaves were brought to Brazil. The average annual importation of slaves during this period was around 30,000. Filas were used to guard the slaves, often over 200 per plantation, and to discourage escape. If a slave did escape, the Filas were used to track them down. Unlike their ancestor, the Bloodhound, the Fila Brasileiro will grab and hold at the end of the trail. The word "*fila*" actually translates into "to hold" in the old Portuguese language. Slavery ended in 1888 in Brazil, but the Fila continued to perform many other duties.

The early Filas also served as hunting dogs. Filas were used for centuries to hunt large prey, such as wild boar and jaguars. The dense jungles of Brazil posed little problem for these robust dogs, which were even able to withstand the assaults of mosquitoes and other insects that inhabit the jungle. The Fila Brasileiro also

Filas are used for guarding large plantations in their homeland. Ideal for this type of work, they are highly protective and very suspicious of strangers.

PHOTO BY DR HERBERT R AXELROD

In 1960 Dr. Herbert R. Axelrod, the tropical fish explorer, took HRH King Leopold of Belgium into the jungle to visit a remote tribe of pygmies. They had several Filas that they stole from cattle ranches (*fazendas*). It is common for cattle to be placed on one of the thousands of islands in the Amazon-Rio Negro rivers. A caretaker watches them and visits the island every few days. A Fila may be left with the cattle to chase alligators, poachers, jaguars and snakes.

put his hunting skills to use on the large ranches of Brazil, protecting the livestock and ranch owners.

These large ranches employed many Filas, not only as livestock guardians but also as cattle drovers. A powerful, trustworthy dog was needed to drive the cattle over the open areas of Brazil. The Fila Brasileiro has a natural herding instinct, much like his abilities as a guard dog.

The Fila Brasileiro's natural dislike of strangers, coupled with a proverbial faithfulness to his master, made it a natural choice as a guard dog for the people of Brazil. As time went on, and more people were moving to the big cities, the Filas went with them. The Filas' aggressiveness toward burglars made them a popular choice with property owners in the cities. The modern Fila Brasileiro exhibits this same temperament toward strangers and is a popular choice for a guard dog today.

INTRODUCTION TO COUNTRIES OUTSIDE BRAZIL

The first European country to notice the Fila was Germany,

which already had a history of interest in guardian breeds. In 1953, Prince Albrecht von Bayern imported the first Fila Brasileiro to Germany. It is said that he had become interested in the Fila during an earlier excursion to Brazil. He later imported several Fila bitches. Thus, the popularity of the Fila began to grow in Germany, and other countries would soon take an interest as well. When the FCI officially recognized the Fila Brasileiro breed in 1968, the standard was introduced in England, Holland and Italy, but it would be another decade before the Fila would really get noticed.

The 1980s was a very important decade in the history of the Fila Brasileiro outside Brazil. One of the most significant books on the Fila Brasileiro was published in 1981. *Grande Livro do Fila Brasileiro*, written by Procópio do Valle, is one of the finest volumes on the Fila Brasileiro ever written. Half of the copies printed were sold abroad.

During the 1980s, hundreds of Filas were sent to countries

Philo do Camping, at six months of age, showing off her excellent scenting abilities and a typical "Fila pace."

around the world, including
Nigeria, Japan and South Africa.
The Fila was also gaining popularity all over Europe. The interest
was growing in the Netherlands,
Austria, Portugal, Spain and
Hungary, later to be followed by
Belgium and Sweden. It was
around the same time (1979) that
the first litter of Filas was born in
the United States. The Fila's
popularity continues to spread in
each of these countries as more
and more fanciers discover the
alluring qualities of the majestic
Fila Brasileiro.

FORMATION OF BREED CLUBS
As the popularity of the Fila
Brasileiro grew, clubs dedicated to
the breed began to appear. The
first Fila Brasileiro specialty club
in Brazil, *El Associacao do Fila
Brasileiro do Estado do Rio de
Janeiro* (AFBERJ), was founded by
Jacob and Andrea Blumen in the
1970s. AFBERJ is still an active
club dedicated to the betterment
of the breed. Numerous state
clubs for the Fila Brasileiro were
founded in the 1980s in Brazil.

As interest in the Fila
Brasileiro spread to other countries, clubs were started to
promote the breed abroad. The
Fila Brasileiro Club of America
(FBCA) was founded in 1984 by a
small group of Fila fanciers. The
FBCA, headquartered in the state
of Georgia, maintains a stud book
and registry. This club is still

Philo do Camping,
at age 15 months,
chases squirrels up
a tree. Filas are
usually intolerant
of any trespassers
whether they are
humans or
animals.

The head of a lovely black Fila. This bitch is named Madie.

several European delegates covering Belgium, Luxembourg, Hungary, Finland, Portugal and the Netherlands. Besides the many delegates throughout Europe and the United States, the FBA is represented in Brazil, Colombia, Mexico, New Zealand, Costa Rica, Honduras and the West Indies.

Most of the clubs covering the Fila Brasileiro in Europe are not specialty clubs; that is, they are not dedicated to only one breed. In Europe, clubs that promote the Fila Brasileiro usually represent other breeds as well. One example of this type of club is Portugal's *Clube Portugues do Molossos de Arena*, which covers the Fila Brasileiro, Neapolitan Mastiff, Mastiff, Bullmastiff and Dogue de Bordeaux. Other European clubs include: Germany's *Der Club für Molosser*, the Netherlands'

active in the United States.

Another club founded in the United States is the Fila Brasileiro Association (FBA). Clelia Kruel, CBKC/FCI/SKC judge and Fila Brasileiro breeder, founded the FBA in 1992. The FBA follows the policies of *Confederação Brasileira de Cinofilia* (CBKC), which is the official organization in Brazil affiliated with the FCI. Though the FBA is headquartered in the United States, it is an international organization and one of the largest Fila specialty clubs in the world. The FBA currently has

GENUS *CANIS*

Dogs and wolves are members of the genus *Canis*. Wolves are known scientifically as *Canis lupus* while dogs are known as *Canis domesticus*. Dogs and wolves are known to interbreed. The term "canine" derives from the Latin derived word *Canis*. The term "dog" has no scientific basis but has been used for thousands of years. The origin of the word "dog" has never been authoritatively ascertained.

Nederlandse Mastino Napoletano en Molosser Club, Austria's *Österreichscher Klub für Grosse Hunderassen* and Spain's *Club Español de los Molosos de Arena*. As the popularity of the Fila Brasileiro grows, we may see more specialty clubs dedicated solely to the Fila Brasileiro in Europe.

If you plan on getting a Fila Brasileiro, it is a good idea to join (at least one) of these clubs. Any one of these Fila Brasileiro clubs can provide you with valuable information on the breed, as well as provide contacts with Fila breeders and owners who can help answer any question you may have. Most clubs put out regular newsletters that are mailed to all members. Members can post show results, announce litters and exchange information in these newsletters.

Another concern that many clubs are facing is defeating breed-specific legislation. This type of legislation, usually brought on by panic and misinformation, seeks to ban certain breeds, especially those breeds related to fighting dogs and other "dangerous" dogs. In many areas, the Fila Brasileiro is included in this list of so-called "dangerous" breeds. Some countries have already successfully passed such laws. For example, the Fila Brasileiro is banned in England under the Dangerous Dog Act, the

White is allowed on the chest, toes and tip of the tail. The rear of the dog is higher than the front.

same legislation that banned the American Pit Bull Terrier, Tosa Inu and Dogo Argentino.

THE FILA'S POPULARITY TODAY

Though the Fila Brasileiro is still considered a rare breed, its popularity continues to rise. The number of puppies being registered in Brazil does not match those of the early 1980s (when the popularity of the Fila Brasileiro reached its apex), but we must remember that many Filas are now being registered outside

Filas are excellent guard dogs and they can be trained (by experts) to protect their owners against any type of physical attack. Filas have an inborn suspicion of strangers. For pet owners, this may not be the most desirable characteristic of their temperament.

Brazil. The numbers in the United States are growing at a rapid pace.

In Europe, the growing popularity of the breed is evident at the dog shows. We see more and more Fila owners participating in shows and some countries hosting Fila Brasileiro specialty shows. Luxembourg, Italy, Hungary and Germany have all seen good participation from Fila owners at recent shows. Some European countries face battles over laws seeking to ban the Fila Brasileiro, but others are enjoying the rising popularity of the breed in their areas.

The growing acceptance of the breed is also evident in the good placements the Fila Brasileiro has

Though many Fila Brasileiro fanciers are happy to see the interest in the breed expand, they are also worried. With popularity comes many other things—more "commercial" breeders, more uninformed buyers and more health problems in the breed. Commercial breeders only breed to make money; they do not care about improving the Fila Brasileiro. Any caring Fila breeder can tell you that you will not get rich breeding Filas; it costs a lot of money to properly care for the dam and her puppies, and a lot of time to research possible families for your Fila pups. We can only hope that honest, selective breeders will continue to breed high-quality, healthy Filas and strive to better the breed.

BRAIN AND BRAWN

Since dogs have been inbred for centuries, their physical and mental characteristics are constantly being changed to suit man's desires for hunting, retrieving, scenting, guarding and warming their masters' laps. During the past 150 years, dogs have been judged according to physical characteristics as well as functional abilities. Few breeds can boast a genuine balance between physique, working ability and temperament.

been receiving at recent shows. Until recently, a Fila Brasileiro would be considered fortunate to be awarded a Group first or second. As breed acceptance has grown and judges have become more familiar with the breed, Filas have been awarded Best in Show and received many international distinctions.

FILA BRASILEIRO

"FAITHFUL AS A FILA"

The Fila Brasileiro's dedication to his master is legendary, as we can see in the Brazilian saying "Faithful as a Fila." Who is this dog that inspired the Brazilian proverb?

THE UNIQUE TEMPERAMENT OF THE FILA BRASILEIRO

Just as the Fila's loyalty towards his family is unsurpassed, so is his dislike for strangers. The Fila has a "dual personality" of sorts and is one of the few breeds in which temperament is so important that breeders commonly regard it as more important than physical traits. This is one of the main things that sets the Fila Brasileiro apart from many other breeds.

The Fila Brasileiro's official standard is very specific about his character and temperament: "Outstanding courage, determination and bravery are part of his characteristics. He is docile and obedient to his owners and family and extremely tolerant with children. His faithfulness became a Brazilian proverb. He is always looking for the company of his master. One of his characteristics is his *ojeriza* (bad will) towards

strangers. He shows a calm disposition, self-assurance and self-confidence, not being disturbed by strange noises nor when facing a new environment. An unsurpassed guardian of property, he is also inclined, by instinct, to hunt big game and to herd cattle." Let us examine the different aspects of the Fila's temperament, as written in the breed standard.

Courage, determination and bravery are evident in the Fila Brasileiro from a very young age. Fila puppies as young as eight weeks old will bravely investigate new objects placed in front of them. Young puppies will also bark at strange noises, always investigating without hesitation. A Fila should never show cowardice or fear. Cowardice is aptly listed as a disqualification in the breed standard.

Another disqualifying trait is aggression towards his owner. A Fila should always be docile toward his owners and family. It is a myth that the Fila Brasileiro is not good with children; it is quite the opposite. A Fila is very tolerant of his family's children.

The devotion that inspired the Brazilian proverb well describes the Filas of today. The Fila

Filas' dedication to the well-being of their masters (mistresses) is so famous in Brazil that it spawned the expression "Faithful as a Fila." Nobody is going to upset this little girl as long as her Fila is around.

Brasileiro is happiest in the company of his master and will follow him around, content to lay his heavy head in his lap or sleep at his feet. Unlike some other guardian breeds, Filas are not reserved; they are very loving and affectionate with their families.

One of the most important aspects of the Fila Brasileiro is his *ojeriza* towards strangers. *Ojeriza* is a Portuguese word meaning "bad will against someone, dislike, aversion, hate." The Fila Brasileiro harbors these feelings towards all strangers, including children, neighbors, your friends, people on the street. It is up to the Fila's owner to temper these feelings with training and proper socialization. That does not mean that you will get rid of the *ojeriza*. This is the Fila Brasileiro's natural temperament and should not be eliminated by training or selective breeding.

Though the Fila Brasileiro has strong feelings towards strangers, he should nevertheless show a calm disposition. A Fila is self-confident in any situation, never hesitating to take on a challenge or face a new environment.

Because of his self-assurance and dislike towards strangers, the Fila Brasileiro makes an exceptional and natural guardian. The Fila does not require special training to learn to protect his family and property. He is very territorial and will protect any territory he is placed in, whether it is a pen, your car or any other area. This territoriality will extend to very large areas as well. Filas can be found protecting vast estates or working on large ranches.

Not only can Filas work as guardians on farms, they also can be used to herd or drove livestock. The Fila Brasileiro is a true working breed with a natural herding instinct.

Though the Fila Brasileiro is inclined to hunt big game, he usually gets along with other dogs and animals. Many Filas live in multi-pet households and can easily make friends with other animals with whom they are raised. They may, however, try to "hunt" strange animals that come into their territory.

A Fila Brasileiro is truly an extraordinary dog with many different sides. He can be a sentry one minute, a teddy bear the next. He is what you want him to be, with few limitations. His appearance, of course, is equally as distinctive and impressive as his personality.

WHAT DOES A FILA LOOK LIKE?

The Fila Brasileiro is a typical molosser breed. The Fila's short, smooth coat can be any solid color except white, mouse gray, patched, dappled or black and tan. Brindles are allowed in any of the basic colors, with stripes of

This giant Fila couldn't be more content, with his mistress and a tasty rawhide bone. This male is almost 150 lb and his superior guardian instincts remain unchallenged!

The dam, all dressed up, with her white-toed puppy.

varying intensities. A black mask may or may not be present and white markings are only desirable on the feet, chest and tip of tail.

One of the Fila Brasileiro's most important characteristics is the thick, loose skin that covers the entire body. At the neck, this loose skin forms pronounced dewlaps. Folds may also be present on the chest and abdomen, and some dogs show a fold at the sides of the head. Though wrinkles should not be seen on the Fila's head while in repose, they may be present when alert.

Males stand up to 30 inches tall. The female Fila Brasileiro, which shows a femininity that is immediately recognizable, is about 2 inches shorter. Unlike most other large breeds, the Fila Brasileiro is surprisingly agile. A Fila can easily scale a wall of 6 feet, which is no small feat for a dog that weighs over 100 lb. Filas are also very flexible and can touch their nose to their rear, almost bending themselves in half.

The Fila Brasileiro's almond-shaped eyes are large and spaced well apart on his massive, heavy head. The eye color ranges from dark chestnut to yellow, but is always in harmony with the color of the coat.

The ears of the Fila Brasileiro are large and pendant, broad at the base and tapering at the end. The top of the ears should be

The famous Fila gait is more like that of a stalking lion than a dog.

What could be better than to raise a kid and a puppy together? The Fila is a complicated dog to raise and should absolutely not be the first dog you own.

level with the eyes when at rest; when alert, the ears are held higher on the head. The ears are drooping at the cheeks. "Rose ear"—which is also typical in the breed—is when the ears are held folded back, allowing the interior to be seen.

Another distinguishing char-acteristic of the Fila Brasileiro is the "camel pace." The natural pace is a two-beat lateral gait, in which both legs on one side move together as a pair. This causes a rocking motion of the body. The Fila Brasileiro's forelimbs are shorter than the hind legs, so he stands lower in the withers than in the croup. The Fila also has the ability to drop between the shoul-ders when trailing or crouching. This gives the Fila Brasileiro the appearance of the big cats.

IS THE FILA BRASILEIRO THE BREED FOR YOU?

The decision to get any dog is a big one. The decision to get a big dog is a giant one. When that big dog is the Fila Brasileiro, you are making one of life's great deci-sions. Proceed with caution, *señor y señora.* You need to seriously examine yourself and your living situation to see if the Fila Brasileiro will fit into your lifestyle.

The Fila Brasileiro is not the dog for a first-time dog owner. An inexperienced owner will not have the knowledge or skill to deal with the intelligence, stub-bornness and strong will of the Fila. In order to keep the sharp temperament of the Fila under control, you should have experi-ence with other working and/or guardian breeds.

Fila owners must be strong enough to show the Fila that they

The crouching cat-like walk raises the backside higher than the head. This is a typical Fila characteristic.

are the "Alphas," the leaders of the pack. The Fila Brasileiro needs to have respect for his owner and know his place in the "pack order" of his family.

Like the size of the Fila Brasileiro, the responsibility you have as a Fila owner is giant. Because of the Fila's natural *ojeriza*, you need to be aware of your surroundings at all times. You cannot let your Fila run free; he must always be under your control, in all situations. You need to be willing and able to take on this responsibility.

If you have many different people coming in and out of your life, then you may want to consider another breed. Filas do not like strangers; that includes

The size and activity level of a Fila are two gigantic considerations. Standing on his toes, the Fila is as tall as some people. Are you capable of controlling such a creature?

anyone that is a stranger to the dog, even if he or she is a friend of yours. You need to realize that the Fila Brasileiro is not a dog that will give your friends slobbery kisses. Will you be able to make accommodations for your Fila when people come to visit? You need to be prepared for any situation that may arise.

Another consideration is your activity level. Unlike some of the other large breeds, the Fila Brasileiro is not a sedentary animal. As a working dog, the Fila requires activity and mental stimulation. Owners must dedicate at least two hours per day to entertaining and exercising the Fila. If you are a quiet homebody who never seeks outdoor-type activity, you are not a Fila candidate.

If you have decided that you are the right type of person to own a Fila Brasileiro and are willing to commit the time and energy to train and socialize him properly, then consider your surroundings.

A Fila is a large working dog that needs an ample area in which to live. If you live in a small apartment, the Fila Brasileiro is not the breed for you. You will at least need to have a large yard with very secure fencing. Filas can live inside or outside; they are very tolerant and can live in warm or cold climates. While many "dog people" cringe at the thought of a dog living outside, the Fila is a very different, durable and independent creature. Yes, it can live and thrive outdoors—this, of

The Fila is a working dog that needs a lot of room in which to exercise and live. If you live in a small apartment or condo, do not consider owning a Fila.

Fazenda do Indomito's Basra, owned by Camping Kennels and bred by Fazenda do Indomito Kennels, was certified with excellent hips. Both her parents had good hips. Most European pedigrees show the hip ratings, which is helpful to breeders and new puppy owners.

course, does not mean without attention from his master!

If you decide that you are the right type of person to own a Fila, you will discover that having a Fila Brasileiro is not only a huge responsibility but also a great joy. The bond formed between a Fila and his owner is truly remarkable. Few breeds will show you the affection and dedication that the Fila can. As the owner of a Fila Brasileiro, you will know the true meaning of "Faithful as a Fila."

BREED-SPECIFIC HEALTH CONCERNS
As a large breed, the Fila Brasileiro is more prone to certain health problems, and these are things that a new owner should consider when making the deci-

sion to own and care for a Fila. Canine hip dysplasia and bloat are two conditions that are more common in the breed. There are things you can do as a responsible owner to help prevent both of these conditions.

HIP DYSPLASIA
The term *dysplasia* means an alteration in size, shape or organization. Hip dysplasia is defined as an alteration in size, shape or organization of the hip joint. The canine hip joint, like a human hip joint, is made up of a ball and socket. When a hip joint is dysplastic, there are alterations in the perfect symmetry of the ball and socket. This could be an improper fit, a flattening of the ball portion or a shallowing of the

socket portion. The imperfection can lead to joint malfunction, which can lead to arthritic changes. The body tries to stabilize the joint by building bony bridges, leading to osteoarthritis.

Canine hip dysplasia is an inherited trait that is influenced by several genes. It is more common in large, rapidly growing dogs like the Fila Brasileiro. Though hip dysplasia is not caused by environmental factors, environment can instigate or worsen the progression of the disease.

The first thing you can do to prevent your Fila from getting hip dysplasia is to buy your puppy from a good breeder. Reputable breeders should have all breeding stock x-rayed and checked for hip dysplasia. Buying a puppy whose parents are free of hip dysplasia is your first defense against the disabling condition. Breeders should follow certain guidelines to decrease the incidence of hip dysplasia in a breeding program: breed normal to normal, breed normals with normal ancestry, breed normals from litters with low incidence of hip dysplasia and select a sire that produces a low incidence of hip dysplasia.

Some environmental factors that can worsen hip dysplasia are rough play, jumping, climbing stairs or being kept on slippery floors. Excess weight gain (especially during the first year of life) or rapid growth and excess calcium supplementation can also worsen the disease. Breeders who are aware of environmental factors use non-slip matting for their whelping boxes, as experience has proven that big-boned puppies can damage growing ligaments by slipping and falling about in their whelping pens.

You should keep your Fila Brasileiro puppy lean, avoid any type of forced exercise or very rough play and provide surfaces that allow for good traction. You should wait until your puppy is at least seven months old to do any running on asphalt (or other hard surfaces).

BLOAT (GASTRIC DILATATION/VOLVULUS)

Bloat is a term that is synonymous with the scientific term "gastric dilatation/volvulus." It is often called GDV. The dog's stomach distends with air to the point that the dog goes into shock and may die. Dilatation means that the stomach is distended with air, but it is still located in the abdomen in its correct place. Volvulus means that the distention is associated with a twisting of the stomach.

Bloat was originally thought to occur when a dog ate a large meal of dry food and then drank a lot of water. The water caused the dry food to swell. Strenuous exercise, like running and jumping, after eating was thought to be another factor. The result was the dog's stomach twisting on itself as it was shaken around in the abdomen. Vets identify the cause of bloat to be the swallowing of air, usually when a dog is gulping his food. Bloat almost always occurs in deep-chested dogs of large breeds, like the Fila Brasileiro.

To help prevent bloat, vets recommend feeding your dog two or three smaller meals a day (rather than one large meal) and feeding at a time when the dog can be observed after they have eaten. Feeding wet food (canned or moistened dry food) is also thought to help prevent bloat. Feed your dog in a quiet location and avoid exercise, excitement and stress one hour before and two hours after eating (walking is allowed, because it helps stimulate normal gastrointestinal function). If you have more than one

dog, you should feed them separately. Provide water for your dog at all times except feeding time. Some vets have proposed purchasing elevated bowl stands so that the Fila is not stretching his neck to eat. Many breeders endorse this idea.

Some symptoms of bloat may be anxiety, evidence of abdominal fullness after meals, heavy salivating, whining, pacing, getting up and lying down, stretching, looking at the abdomen, unproductive attempts to vomit, labored breathing, disinterest in food and a stilted gait. Severe symptoms include dark red, blue, gray or white gums, a rapid heartbeat and a weak pulse. You should call your veterinarian at the first signs of bloat. If your dog is in the late stages of bloat, you may need to administer first aid on the way to the veterinary hospital. You may want to discuss emergency procedures with your vet.

Maggie is only ten months old but she gets along well with the pet cat. The cat seems to be comfortable around Maggie, too.

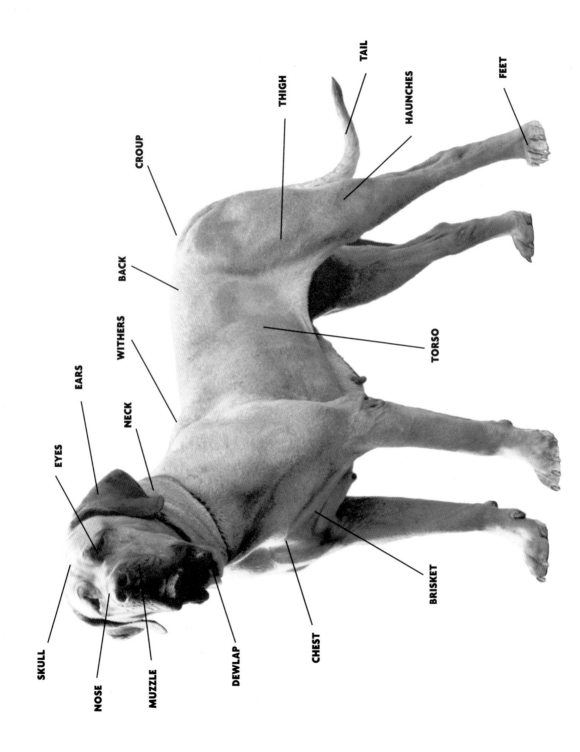

BREED STANDARD FOR THE

FILA BRASILEIRO

THE FILA BRASILEIRO OFFICIAL FCI STANDARD
translated by CBKC/FCI/SKC Judge Clelia Kruel

GENERAL APPEARANCE

Typically molossoid breed with powerful bones, rectangular and compact structure but harmonious and proportional. Added to his massiveness a great agility can be easily seen. Bitches must show a well-defined femininity, which differentiates them immediately from males.

CHARACTER AND TEMPERAMENT

Outstanding courage, determination and bravery are part of his characteristics. He is docile and obedient to his owners and family and extremely tolerant with children. His faithfulness became a Brazilian proverb. He is always looking for the company of his master. One of his characteristics is his *ojeriza* towards strangers. He shows a calm disposition, self-assurance and self-confidence, not being disturbed by strange noises nor when facing a new environment. An unsurpassed guardian of property, he is also inclined, by instinct, to hunt big game and to herd cattle.

GAIT

The Fila has a long reach and elastic gait which reminds one of the great cats' movements. His main characteristic is the pace (camel's gait), moving two legs of one side first, followed by the two legs of the other side which causes a rolling lateral movement of the thorax and hindquarters accentuated by the tail when it is raised. During the walk he maintains the head lower than the back line. He shows a smooth, free and long-reaching trot with a powerful stride. His gallop is powerful with an unsuspected speed coming from such a large and heavy dog. The Fila Brasileiro's gait is always influenced by its typically molossoid articulations which give the impression, and in fact it is true, of effectively permitting him sudden and swift changes in direction.

EXPRESSION

In repose it is calm, noble and full of self-assurance, never disclosing a bored nor absent expression. When at attention, the expression should reflect determination and alertness with a firm and piercing look in his eyes.

HEAD

The Fila's head is heavy and massive, always proportionate to the body. Seen from above, it resembles a trapezoidal figure in which the head appears pear-shaped. From a side view, muzzle and skull should have approximately the proportion of 1 to 1, or with the first being slightly smaller than the second one.

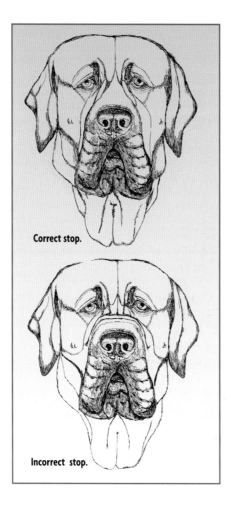

Correct stop.

Incorrect stop.

SKULL

The profile shows a smooth curve from the stop to the occiput, which is well-defined and salient, especially in puppies. From a front view, the skull is wide, ample with the upper line slightly curved. The lateral lines descend slightly curved, almost in a vertical line, narrowing toward the muzzle, never showing a stop.

STOP

From a front view, it is practically non-existent. The medium furrow runs up smoothly until approximately the halfway mark of the skull. From a side view, the stop is low, sloping and virtually formed by the very well-developed eyebrow ridges.

MUZZLE

Strong, broad and deep, always in harmony with the skull. From a top view, it is full under the eyes, very slightly narrowing toward the middle of the muzzle and slightly broadening again until reaching the front curve. From a side view, the bridge of the muzzle is straight or has a Roman nose, but never in an ascendant line. The front line of the muzzle is close to a perpendicular line in relation to the superior line, showing a slight depression right under the nose. A perfect curve is formed by the upper lips, which are thick and pendulous, drooping over the lower lips, giving shape to the lower line of the muzzle, which is almost parallel to the upper line. The labial rim is always apparent. The lower lips are close and firm up to the fangs and from there on they are loose with dented borders. The muzzle has a great depth at the root but without surpassing the length of the muzzle. The labial rim has the shape of an inverted and deep U.

Nose
Well-developed with broad nostrils not occupying entirely the maxilla width. The color is black.

Eyes
From medium to large size, almond-shaped, spaced well apart, from medium to deep-set. The colors are from dark chestnut to yellow, always in harmony with the coat color. Due to the profusion of the loose skin, many individuals present drooping lower eyelids which are not considered a fault as such detail increases the melancholy expression, which is typical of the breed.

Ears
Pendant, large, thick, V-shaped, broad at the base and tapering at the end with rounded tips. They are inserted at the posterior part of the skull in line with the medium level of the eyes when in repose. When roused the ears go above the original position. The

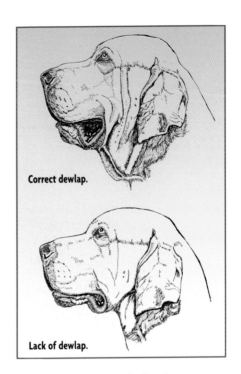

Correct dewlap.

Lack of dewlap.

root is oblique with the front border higher than the back border. The ears are drooping at the cheeks or are folded back allowing the interior to be seen.

Teeth
Noticeably wider than long. They are strong and white. The upper scissors are broad at the root and sharp at the edges. Canines are powerful, well set and well apart. A scissors bite is the ideal, but a level bite is acceptable.

Neck
Extraordinarily strong and well muscled, giving the impression of a short neck. It is slightly curved

on the top and well detached from the skull. The throat is furnished with dewlaps.

TOPLINE
The withers, standing in a sloping line, are set well apart from each other due to the distance between the scapulas at a slightly lower level than the croup. After the withers, the topline changes direction, ascending smoothly to the croup, with no tendency to show a sway nor a roach back.

CROUP
Broad and long, with an approximate angulation of 30 degrees to the horizontal line, showing a

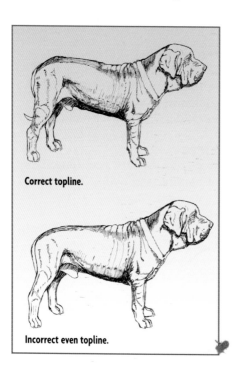

Correct topline.

Incorrect even topline.

smooth curve. It stands a little higher than the withers. Viewed from the rear, the croup must be ample and its width is approximately equal to the thorax and may be even wider in females.

BODY
Strong, broad and deep, covered by thick and loose skin. The thorax is longer than the abdomen. The length of the body is the same as the height at the withers plus 10%, when measured from the point of the shoulder to the point of the buttocks.

THORAX
The ribs are well sprung, though not interfering with the position of the shoulders. The chest is deep and large, descending to the level of the elbows.

LOINS
Shorter and not as deep as the thorax, showing a separation of the two component parts. The lower part of the loins is more developed in the females. Viewed from above, the loins are narrower than the thorax and croup, but should not form a waistline.

UNDERLINE
The chest is long and parallel to the ground in all its extension. The tuck-up extends in a slightly ascending line but is never whippety.

FOREQUARTERS

The ideal shoulder structure should be composed of two bones of equal length (scapula and humerus), with the former at an angle of 45 degrees from the horizontal line and the humerus forming an approximate 90-degree angle with the scapula. The articulation of the scapula-humerus forms the point of the shoulder, which should be situated at the level of the prosternum but a little behind it. In its ideal position the shoulder covers the space from the withers to the prosternum, and the point of the shoulder should be placed halfway to this distance. An imaginary perpendicular line coming down from the withers should cut the elbow and reach the foot.

FORELEGS

Must be parallel, straight to the pasterns, and with powerful bones. The carpus (pastern joints) are strong and apparent. The metacarpus (pasterns) are short and slightly sloping. Length of the leg from ground to elbow should be equal to the length from elbow to withers.

FEET

Formed by strong and well-arched toes, which are not too close together. The pads are thick, broad, and deep. The correct position of the feet is pointing to the front. The nails are strong and

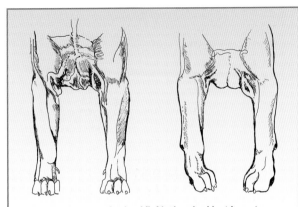

Toes must point straight ahead (left). They should neither point in (pigeon-toed, as shown on right) nor out (splayed).

dark, but they may be white when this is the color of the respective toe.

HINDQUARTERS

The hindlegs are less heavy boned than the forelegs but never light as a whole. The upper thigh has curved borders shaped by muscles descending from the ilium and ischium, which trace the curve of the rear, and for this reason the ischium must have a good length.

HINDLEGS

Parallel, with strong tarsus, metatarsus slightly bent, higher than the metacarpus. The stifles and hocks are moderately angulated.

HINDFEET

A little more oval than the forefeet, but otherwise the description is identical to that for

Good rear.

Poor rear, cowhocks.

the forefeet. They should not present dewclaws.

TAIL
Very wide at the root, medium set, reaching to the level of the hocks, tapering rapidly at its end. When the dog is alert, the tail is raised high, and the curve at the extremity is more accentuated. The tail should not fall over the back or curl up.

HEIGHT
Measured at the withers: Males: 65 to 75 cms (25.5 to 29.5 in); Females: 60 to 70 cms (23.5 to 27.5 in).

WEIGHT
Males: minimum of 50 kgs (110 lb); Females: minimum of 40 kgs (88 lb).

COLOR
All solid colors are permitted except the disqualifying ones (white, mouse gray, patched dogs, dappled, or black and tan). Brindles of a basic color may have the stripes of either less or with very strong intensity. A black mask may or may not be present. In all permitted colors white markings should be limited to the feet, chest, and tip of tail. The white markings are not desirable on any other part of the body.

SKIN
One of the most important breed characteristics is the thick, loose skin over the whole body, chiefly at the neck, forming pronounced dewlaps, and in many individuals the folds proceed to the chest and abdomen. Some dogs show a fold at the side of the head and also at the withers descending to the shoulder. When the dog is in repose, the head is free of wrinkles. When alert, in order to lift the ears, the contraction of the skin at the skull forms little wrinkles along a longitudinal line of the skull.

COAT
Short, smooth, dense and tight to the skin.

TEST OF TEMPERAMENT
This is compulsory requirement for all individuals (after 12 months) in order to obtain a registered championship title.

All champions must have a certificate of approval at the

temperament test. This type of test is made at all specialty shows. It is optional at general shows, up to the judge's will, providing it is public and takes place outside the show ring.

The trial includes:

1. Attack with a stick. The dog is supposed to attack in front of the handler, without being coached, and the exhibitor or handler will remain in his position. It is forbidden to touch or to beat the animal.

2. Shooting test. There will be blanks fired at a distance of five meters from the dog. The dog should express attention, show self-confidence and self-assurance.

3. During all performances in the ring, the judge will analyze the behavior and temperament of the entrant, paying attention to his expression. During the temperament test, the following should be observed:

    The dislike of the animal to strangers.

    The self-assurance, courage, determination, and bravery of each dog.

FAULTS

General Faults:
Cryptorchid or monorchid, the use of artificial products, or a dog which has been changed in appearance by artificial means, albinos, lack of type, etc.

Disqualifications:
1. Aggressiveness toward his owner
2. Cowardice
3. Pink nose
4. Overshot bite
5. Undershot bite showing the teeth when the mouth is closed
6. Lack of one canine or one molar, other than the third one
7. Blue eyes (porcelain like)
8. Cropped ears or docked tail

Wrinkled skin, especially around the neck, is a highly desirable characteristic of the Fila.

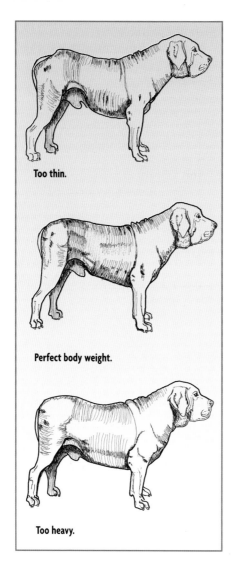

Too thin.

Perfect body weight.

Too heavy.

Looking at the Fila from above, you can see the thin animal at the left, the ideal-weight animal in the centre, and the heavy animal to the right. Filas must be heavy, but the weight should come from muscle not fat.

9. Croup lower than the withers
10. All dogs that are white, mouse gray, patched, dappled or merle or black and tan
11. Under minimum height
12. Lack of loose skin
13. Lack of camel's pace

Very Serious Faults:
1. Small head
2. Tight upper lips
3. A pronounced stop from a front view
4. Protruding eyes
5. Lack of two teeth except the PIS (first pre-molars)
6. Lack of dewlaps
7. Apathetic or timid dogs
8. Negative sensitivity to shooting a gun
9. Roach back
10. Level topline
11. Excessive tuckup
12. Cowhocks

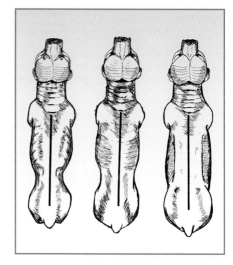

13. Straight hocks (lack of angulation at the hindlegs)
14. Light bones
15. Lack of substance
16. Over maximum height
17. White markings exceeding one-quarter of the body
18. Lack of pigmentation at eye rim
19. Round eyes
20. Square figure

Serious Faults:
1. Short muzzle
2. Small ears
3. High set ears (when in repose)
4. Excessively light colored eyes
5. Wrinkles on skull when the animal is in repose
6. Undershot bite
7. Lack of two teeth
8. Folded skin under throat that is not dewlap
9. Swayback

10. Narrow croup
11. A curled tail carried over the back
12. Chest lacking depth
13. Deviation of metacarpus or metatarsus
14. Over-angulated hindlegs
15. Short steps

Minor Faults:
Anything in disagreement with the standard that does not fall into the above three categories

NOTE
Male animals should have two apparently normal testicles fully descended into the scrotum.

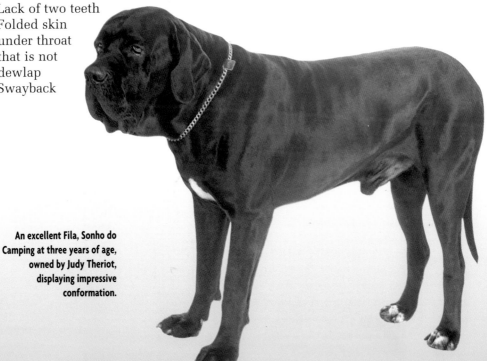

An excellent Fila, Sonho do Camping at three years of age, owned by Judy Theriot, displaying impressive conformation.

FILA BRASILEIRO

BEFORE BRINGING A PUPPY HOME

There are many things you must consider before making the final decision to get a Fila. The Fila Brasileiro is definitely not the dog for everyone. It is a unique breed with a strong temperament and it requires a special kind of owner. This is not a breed for first-time dog owners. If you are someone who has experience with other guardian or working breeds, then consider these other owner requirements.

RESPONSIBILITY

Owning a Fila is a full-time responsibility, not just for the first few months of puppyhood, but for the life of the dog. The Fila is on guard 24 hours a day. The breed's unique temperament means that you must always be aware of your dog and your surroundings. This is not a dog that can run around the neighborhood; you must have complete control over your Fila at all times. Besides the special responsibilities that a Fila brings, there is also the responsibility of meeting your puppy's basic needs.

Before you acquire a Fila, you need to decide who will have primary responsibility for his daily care. Your puppy looks to his human owners for all his needs. Who will feed him? Who will let him outside? Discuss it

Opposite page: While many attributes of the Fila are attractive, not the least of which are his puppy cuteness and faithful character, there are many serious considerations in the acquisition of such a giant, powerful and aggressive dog.

ARE YOU PREPARED?

Unfortunately, when a puppy is bought by someone who does not take into consideration the time and attention that dog ownership requires, it is the puppy who suffers when he is either abandoned or placed in a shelter by a frustrated owner. So all of the "homework" you do in preparation for your pup's arrival will benefit you both. The more informed you are, the more you will know what to expect and the better equipped you will be to handle the ups and downs of raising a puppy. Hopefully, everyone in the household is willing to do his part in raising and caring for the pup. The anticipation of owning a dog often brings a lot of promises from excited family members: "I will walk him every day," "I will feed him," "I will house-train him," etc., but these things take time and effort, and promises can easily be forgotten once the novelty of the new pet has worn off.

with your family to see who can take on certain duties. Make sure that all family members are included in the decision to acquire a Fila Brasileiro. Everyone must agree on the adopting of the dog, or this likely will lead to problems later.

PROVIDING A SECURE AREA

A Fila Brasileiro is a large, powerful dog. It is an absolute requirement that you have a secure area for your Fila. A Fila can easily live on a farm or ranch, but can also be kept in a residential area if you have a large property. However, you must have secure fencing. It should be at least 6 feet high to accommo-

date an adult Fila and not have any gaps where a Fila puppy could escape.

If you have a special area of the house where your Fila puppy will be kept, make sure that it does not have slippery floors (such as hardwood or linoleum). Keeping your Fila puppy on a slick floor can cause him to slip, which can lead to problems with his legs, including fallen pasterns and possibly hip dysplasia. If your house has a lot of bare floors, you will probably want to purchase some large area rugs or carpeting for these areas.

SOCIALIZATION AND TRAINING

A Fila Brasileiro requires both socialization and training as a puppy. Some people think it is possible to "over-socialize" your Fila puppy, such as having every stranger you meet touch and play with the puppy. They believe this will hinder his abilities as a guard dog later. You should not let this stop you from exposing your Fila Brasileiro puppy to many new situations and people. A Fila is what you want him to be. If you plan on showing your Fila or putting him in other situations where he will be in close proximity to strangers, then you will need to socialize him more. The judge at a dog show is a stranger to your Fila, yet he needs to

TEMPERAMENT COUNTS

Your selection of a good puppy can be determined by your needs. A show potential or a good pet? It is your choice. Every puppy, however, should be of good temperament. Although show-quality puppies are bred and raised with emphasis on physical conformation, responsible breeders strive for equally good temperament. Do not buy from a breeder who concentrates solely on physical beauty at the expense of personality.

Lucy and Philo get along very well together. As a matter of fact, here it seems like Lucy, the Scottish Terrier, is the leader.

come close to the dog to examine him, and even touch him at some shows. At other shows, Filas are not to be penalized for not letting a judge touch them, but they must still tolerate the judge. When your puppy is young, you will need to spend the time taking him out in public and showing him what is and what is not acceptable behavior to you.

Your puppy will also need obedience training. Do you have time to train your Fila Brasileiro? Some of the naughty things your Fila does as a puppy may seem cute, but if you do not start teaching him immediately, you will have over 100 lb of dog that will fly out of control. You must set aside ten minutes or so each day to start teaching your puppy.

FINANCIAL CONSIDERATIONS
Caring for a Fila Brasileiro puppy requires more than your time—it requires *dinero*. You

PUPPY APPEARANCE
Your puppy should have a well-fed appearance but not a distended abdomen, which may indicate worms or incorrect feeding, or both. The body should be firm, with a solid feel. The skin of the abdomen should be pale pink and clean, without signs of scratching or rash. Check the hind legs to make certain that dewclaws were removed, if any were present at birth.

Make sure your chosen Fila pup welcomes handling and does not seem overly suspicious or fearful. You don't want a puppy who rejects you or resists human contact. Note how well the front feet point forward.

will have to consider the extra expenses you will incur. Your puppy will need to visit the veterinarian for injections and checkups. Besides health expenses, feeding a high-quality diet to such a huge dog can become very costly.

In fact, everything is more

expensive for a dog as *grande* as the Fila Brasileiro! You will need an extra-large crate, extra-large chew toys, extra-large collars and leads. The prices usually go up with the size, so expect to spend more for Fila-sized items than items for a smaller dog.

ACQUIRING A PUPPY

Once you decide that you meet all the requirements of a responsible Fila owner, you can begin your search for a Fila Brasileiro puppy. Your first step is to start researching kennels. You may want to contact a Fila Brasileiro breed club for a list of breeders in your area. Contact honest, reliable kennels and talk to the breeders. Make sure the breeder has a few generations' experience and is knowledgeable about the breed and willing to

PEDIGREE VS. REGISTRATION CERTIFICATE

Too often new owners are confused between these two important documents. Your puppy's pedigree, essentially a family tree, is a written record of a dog's genealogy of three generations or more. The pedigree will show you the names as well as performance titles of all dogs in your pup's background. Your breeder must provide you with a registration application, with his part properly filled out. You must complete the application and send it to the registry with the proper fee. Every puppy must come from a litter that has been registered by the breeder, and from a sire and dam that are also registered with the same registry.

The seller must provide you with complete records to identify the puppy. The registry usually requires that the seller provide the buyer with the following: breed; sex, color and markings; date of birth; litter number (when available); names and registration numbers of the parents; breeder's name; and date sold or delivered.

answer all of your questions. It is not advisable to buy a Fila from a breeder's first litter! That's not a breeder, it's an experiment!

Ask the breeder about the parents. You want to be certain that the parents have been x-rayed and are free of canine hip dysplasia. Ask for copies of the diagnosis to make sure that this has been legitimately determined. The dogs should also be registered with an organization affiliated with the Fédération Cynologique Internationale (FCI). The breeder should provide you with copies of the parents' pedigrees.

Once you are certain you are dealing with a knowledgeable, supportive breeder, you will want to go meet the litter and see the parents (at least the

Seek out a breeder with an established reputation. Clelia Kruel is a breeder, exhibitor, author and judge whose whole life has been dedicated to Filas. She founded two American Fila clubs and owns the Camping Kennels. She has produced champions for nearly 25 consecutive years.

dam). Because of the temperament of the Fila Brasileiro, you may not be able to get too close to the adult dogs in the kennel. You will want to observe the puppies, even if you cannot meet the dam. The puppies should be alert, active and healthy. They should have clear eyes with no mucus in them. The nose should be a little moist. Also, look at the puppies' coats. Are they soft and shiny? Once you confirm the quality of care that the puppies have received, you can look at the correctness of the pups.

A Fila Brasileiro puppy has a lot of the same characteristics as an adult Fila. The puppies should have massive, heavy heads and strong legs. They also have the characteristic pendu-

PET INSURANCE

Just as you can insure your car, your house and your own health, you likewise can insure your dog's health. Investigate a pet insurance policy by talking to your vet. Depending on the age of your dog, the breed and the kind of coverage you desire, your policy can be very affordable. Most policies cover accidental injuries, poisoning, and thousands of medical problems and illnesses, including cancers. Some carriers also offer routine care and immunization coverage.

Once you have located an experienced breeder whose reputation and puppies meet your approval, you can feel comfortable choosing a puppy. This breeder has two litters on the ground at the same time.

lous lips and dewlap when they are young.

Watch the puppies in motion. They should walk freely with an elastic gait and you should not see any stiffness in the joints. Movement is important, but not the only thing you

YOUR SCHEDULE . . .
If you lead an erratic, unpredictable life, with daily or weekly changes in your work requirements, consider the problems of owning a puppy. The new puppy has to be fed regularly, social-ized (loved, petted, handled, intro-duced to other people) and, most importantly, allowed to go outdoors for house-training. As the dog gets older, he can be more tolerant of deviations in his feeding and relief schedule.

need to observe.

Even at a young age, a Fila puppy is very confident. You will want to avoid a puppy that retreats from unknown objects or is scared by strange sounds. A Fila puppy should walk directly toward and investigate these things. Watch the puppies playing with each other. Look for a cheerful, self-confident puppy.

Do not be overwhelmed by all these things. One reason you chose an experienced, trustwor-thy breeder is so they can help you choose a puppy. Tell the breeder what you want in a dog; he can help you. Do you want a show dog, or are you looking for a companion and watchdog? Maybe you want a working Fila to help you on your farm. Tell the breeder. He knows the breed

If you are lucky enough to find a lovely puppy like this one, don't hesitate to test his personality and physical condition before you acquire it.

TIME TO GO HOME

Breeders rarely release puppies until they are eight to ten weeks of age. This is an acceptable age for most breeds of dog, excepting toy breeds, which are not released until around 12 weeks, given their petite sizes. If a breeder has a puppy that is 12 weeks of age or older, it is likely well socialized and house-trained. Be sure that it is otherwise healthy before deciding to take it home.

intimately and should be able to tell you which puppy should best suit your requirements and lifestyle.

One other thing to consider is whether to get a male or female puppy. Unlike most other breeds, the female Fila Brasileiro is often more aggressive towards strangers. The females are usually easier to train and housebreak. Females will be in season twice a year, while males are always "in season." If you do not intend to show or breed your Fila, you should have him or her neutered, so you will not have to worry about this. Keep in mind that the males are also larger than the females.

A well-adjusted puppy, alert and approachable, is a new owner's best choice for a Fila.

COMMITMENT OF OWNERSHIP

After considering all of these factors, you have most likely already made some very important decisions about selecting your puppy. You have chosen a Fila Brasileiro, which means that you have decided which characteristics you want in a dog and what type of dog will best fit into your family and lifestyle. If you have selected a breeder, you have gone a step further—you have done your research and found a responsible, conscientious person who breeds quality Filas and who should be a reliable source of help as you and your puppy adjust to life together. If you have observed a litter in action, you have obtained a firsthand look at the dynamics of a puppy "pack" and, thus, you have learned about each pup's individual personality—perhaps you have even found one that particularly appeals to you.

However, even if you have not yet found the Fila Brasileiro puppy of your dreams, observing pups will help you learn to recognize certain behaviors and to determine what a pup's behavior indicates about his temperament. You will be able to pick out which pups are the leaders, which ones are less outgoing, which ones are confident, which ones are shy, playful, friendly, aggressive, etc. Equally as important, you will learn to recognize what a healthy pup should look and act like. All of these things will help you in your search, and when you find the Fila

THE RIDE HOME

Taking your dog from the breeder to your home in a car can be a very uncomfortable experience for both of you. The puppy will have been taken from his warm, friendly, safe environment and brought into a strange new environment—an environment that moves! Be prepared for loose bowels, urination, crying, whining and even fear biting. With proper love and encouragement when you arrive home, the stress of the trip should quickly disappear.

Brasileiro that was meant for you, you will know it!

Researching your breed, selecting a responsible breeder and observing as many pups as possible are all important steps on the way to dog ownership. It may seem like a lot of effort... and you have not even brought the pup home yet! Remember, though, you cannot be too careful when it comes to deciding on the dog you want and finding out about your prospective pup's background. Buying a puppy is not—or should not be—just another whimsical purchase. In fact, this is one instance in which you actually do get to choose your own family!

Always keep in mind that a puppy is nothing more than a baby in a furry disguise...a very big baby....who is virtually helpless in a human world and who relies upon his owner for fulfillment of his basic needs for survival. That goes beyond food, water and shelter; your pup needs care, protection, guidance

Five-month-old Philo and Jason. If a picture is worth a thousand words, this picture has a lot to say about the bond between Fila and owner.

FEEDING TIPS
You will probably start feeding your pup the same food that he has been getting from the breeder; the breeder should give you a few days' supply to start you off. Although you should not give your pup too many treats, you will want to have puppy treats on hand for coaxing, training, rewards, etc. Be careful, though, as a small pup's calorie requirements are relatively low and a few treats can add up to almost a full day's worth of calories without the required nutrition.

This is the age at which you ideally should select a Fila puppy—more than 8 weeks old and less than 24 weeks old. A younger pup will neither be properly weaned nor socialized, and an older pup will be more difficult to train and socialize.

QUALITY FOOD

The cost of food must be mentioned. All dogs need a good-quality food with an adequate supply of protein to develop their bones and muscles properly. Most dogs are not picky eaters but, unless fed properly, can quickly succumb to skin problems.

and love. If you are not prepared to commit to this, then you are not prepared to own a dog.

PREPARING PUPPY'S PLACE IN YOUR HOME

Researching your breed and finding a breeder are only two aspects of the "homework" you will have to do before bringing your Fila Brasileiro puppy home. You will also have to prepare your home and family for the new addition. Much as you would prepare a nursery for a newborn baby, you will need to designate a place in your home that will be the puppy's own. How you prepare your home will depend on how much freedom the dog will be allowed: will he be confined to one room or a specific area in the house, or will he be allowed to roam as he pleases? Whatever you decide, you must ensure that he has a place that he can "call his own."

When you bring your new puppy into your home, you are bringing him into what will become his home as well. Obviously, you did not buy a puppy so that he could take over your house, but in order for a puppy to grow into a stable, well-adjusted dog, he has to feel comfortable in his surroundings. Remember, he is leaving the warmth and security of his mother and littermates, plus the familiarity of the only place he has ever known, so it is impor-

PUPPY PROBLEMS

The majority of problems that are commonly seen in young pups will disappear as your dog gets older. However, how you deal with problems when he is young will determine how he reacts to discipline as an adult dog. It is important to establish who is boss (hopefully it will be you!) right away when you are first bonding with your dog. This bond will set the tone for the rest of your life together.

tant to make his transition as easy as possible. It should not take him long to get used to it, but the sudden shock of being transplanted is somewhat trau-

Individual personalities may not be as obvious at this young age, but pups should still show basic Fila qualities of confidence and curiosity. You can draw some conclusions from observing the dam and sire (if possible) and make a judgment about their temperaments and behavior.

matic for a young pup. Imagine how a small child would feel in the same situation—that is how your puppy must be feeling. It is up to you to reassure him and to let him know, "Little *amigo*, you are going to like it here!"

WHAT YOU SHOULD BUY

CRATE

To someone unfamiliar with the use of crates in dog training, it may seem like punishment to shut a dog in a crate; this is not the case at all. Crates are not cruel—crates have many humane and highly effective uses in dog care and training.

PUPPY PROOFING

Thoroughly puppy-proof your house before bringing your puppy home. Never use roach or rodent poisons in any area accessible to the puppy. Avoid the use of toilet bowl cleaners. Most dogs are born with toilet-bowl sonar and will take a drink if the lid is left open. Also keep the trash secured and out of reach.

For example, crate training is a very popular and very successful housebreaking method; a crate can keep your dog safe during travel; and, perhaps most

With his doghouse in the background, this Fila has a ramp so he doesn't have to climb the stairs. Breeders advise limiting young dogs' activity so as not to harm their growing limbs.

importantly, a crate provides your dog with a place of his own in your home. It serves as a "doggie bedroom" of sorts—your Fila Brasileiro can curl up in his crate when he wants to sleep or when he just needs a break. Many dogs sleep in their crates overnight. When lined with soft bedding and a favorite toy, a crate becomes a cozy pseudo-den for your dog. Like his ancestors, he too will seek out the comfort and retreat of a den—you just happen to be providing him with something a little more luxurious than his early ancestors enjoyed.

As far as purchasing a crate, the type that you buy is up to you. It will most likely be one of the two most popular types: wire or fiberglass. There are advantages and disadvantages to each type. For example, a wire

PHOTO COURTESY OF DOSKOCIL.

Crates can be purchased at your local pet shop. Top breeders are convinced that crate training is the best way to housebreak and train a dog. Your pet shop will offer a variety of sizes, styles and colors.

ELECTRIC FENCING

The electrical fencing system which forms an invisible fence works on a battery-operated collar that shocks the dog if he gets too close to the buried (or elevated) wire. There are some people who think very highly of this system of controlling a dog's wandering. Keep in mind that the collar has batteries. For safety's sake, replace the batteries every month with the best quality batteries available.

crate is more open, allowing the air to flow through and affording the dog a view of what is going on around him, while a fiberglass crate is sturdier. Both can double as travel crates, providing protection for the dog. The size of the crate is another thing to consider. Puppies do not stay puppies forever—in fact, sometimes it seems as if they grow right before your eyes. A medium-sized crate may be fine for a very young Fila Brasileiro pup, but it will not do him much good for long! Unless

This small-sized crate is hardly ideal for housing one Fila puppy, no less three or four. Never transport or house more than one puppy in a crate.

your pup home, he has been sleeping amid the warmth of his mother and littermates, and while a blanket is not the same as a warm, breathing body, it still provides heat and something with which to snuggle. You will want to wash your pup's bedding frequently in case he has an accident in his crate and replace or remove any blanket that becomes ragged and starts to fall apart.

Toys

Toys are a must for dogs of all ages, especially for curious playful pups. Puppies are the "children" of the dog world, and what child does not love toys? Chew toys provide enjoyment to both dog and owner—your dog will enjoy playing with his favorite toys, while you will

you have the money and the inclination to buy a new crate every time your pup has a growth spurt, it is better to get one that will accommodate your dog both as a pup and at full size. An extra-large crate, the largest size that you can buy, will be necessary for a full-grown Fila Brasileiro.

You need the largest crate possible for the Fila. They outgrow crates at an alarming rate. This crate will only suit this young pup for a couple of weeks!

BEDDING

A crate pad in the dog's crate will help the dog feel more at home. This will take the place of the leaves, twigs, and so forth that the pup would use in the wild to make a den; the pup can make his own "burrow" in the crate. Although your pup is far removed from his den-making ancestors, the denning instinct is still a part of his genetic makeup. Second, until you bring

Your pet shop will carry many essential items for your Fila Brasileiro, including toys, grooming supplies, crates, bowls and more. Dog ownership is an expensive proposition.

stuffed toys with small plastic eyes or parts that the pup could swallow. Similarly, squeaky toys are quite popular. There are dogs that will come running from anywhere in the house at the first sound from their favorite squeaky friend, but if a pup de-stuffs one of these, the small plastic squeaker inside can be dangerous if swallowed. Monitor the condition of your pup's toys carefully and get rid of any that have been chewed to the point of becoming

enjoy the fact that they distract him from your expensive shoes and leather sofa. Puppies love to chew; in fact, chewing is a physical need for pups as they are teething, and everything looks appetizing! The full range of your possessions—from old dishcloth to Oriental rug—are fair game in the eyes of a teething pup. Puppies are not all that discerning when it comes to finding something to literally "sink their teeth into"— everything tastes great!

Stuffed toys are another option; these are good to put in the dog's crate to give him some company. Be careful of these, as a pup can de-stuff one pretty quickly, and stay away from

CRATE-TRAINING

During crate training, you should partition off the section of the crate in which the pup stays. If he is given too big an area, this will hinder your training efforts. Crate training is based on the fact that a dog does not like to soil his sleeping quarters, so it is ineffective to keep a pup in an area that is so big that he can eliminate in one end and get far enough away from it to sleep. Also, you want to make the crate den-like for the pup. Blankets and a favorite toy will make the crate cozy for the small pup; as he grows, you may want to evict some of his "roommates" to make more room. It will take some coaxing at first, but be patient. Given some time to get used to it, your pup will adapt to his new home-within-a-home quite nicely.

LEAD

A good-sized nylon lead is probably the best option as it is the most resistant to puppy teeth should your pup take a liking to chewing on his lead. Of course, this is a habit that should be nipped in the bud, but if your pup likes to chew on his lead he has a very slim chance of being able to chew through the strong nylon. For everyday walking and safety purposes, the nylon lead is a good choice. There are special leads and harnesses for training purposes, but these are not necessary for routine walks. As your Fila Brasileiro matures, you will want to purchase something stronger, like a thicker leather lead that is designed for large breeds.

COLLAR

Your pup should get used to wearing a collar all the time since you will want to attach his ID tags to his collar. A nylon collar will be a good choice;

With dogs the size of Filas, you need very strong and durable toys. Don't even consider a toy that might be small enough for a Fila to swallow.

potentially dangerous. Consider that the growing Fila needs to be closely supervised whenever he has a destructible toy—and most, if not all, are destructible!

Be careful of natural bones, which have a tendency to splinter into sharp, dangerous pieces. Also be careful of rawhide, which after enough chewing can turn into pieces that are easy to swallow, and also watch out for the mushy mess it can turn into on your carpet. The strongest type nylon bones are recommended for the Fila—-some of these are designed by experts for aggressive-chewing dogs.

STRESS-FREE PUPPY DAYS

Some experts in canine health advise that stress during a dog's early years of development can compromise and weaken his immune system and may trigger the potential for a shortened life. They emphasize the need for happy and stress-free growing-up years.

make sure that it fits snugly enough so that the pup cannot wriggle out of it, but is loose enough so that it will not be uncomfortably tight around the pup's neck. Keep in mind the Fila's abundant neck dewlap. It may take some time for your pup to get used to wearing the collar, but soon he will not even notice that it is there. Choke collars and pinch (or prong) collars are made for training, but should only be used by an owner who knows exactly how to use one. If you use a stronger leather lead or a chain lead to walk your Fila Brasileiro, you will need a heavy-duty leather collar as well.

FOOD AND WATER BOWLS

Your pup will need two bowls, one for food and one for water. You may want two sets of bowls, one for inside and one for outside, depending on where the dog will be fed and where he will be spending most of his time. Stainless steel or sturdy plastic bowls are popular choices. Plastic bowls are more chewable, while dogs tend not to chew on the steel variety, which can also be sterilized. As your Fila grows, it is a good idea to put his food and water bowls on a specially made elevated stand. This brings the food closer to the dog's level so he does not have to bend down

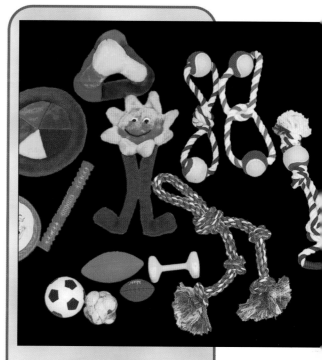

TOYS, TOYS, TOYS!

With a big variety of dog toys available, and so many that look like they would be a lot of fun for a dog, be careful in your selection. It is amazing what a set of puppy teeth can do to an innocent-looking toy, so, obviously, safety is a major consideration. Be sure to choose the most durable products that you can find. Hard nylon bones and toys are a safe bet, and many of them are offered in different scents and flavors that will be sure to capture your dog's attention. It is always fun to play a game of fetch with your dog, and there are balls and flying discs that are specially made to withstand dog teeth.

Pet shops offer dozens of choices for collars and leads, in different styles, colors and lengths. Purchase only the strongest, most durable lead for your Fila.

as far, thus aiding his digestion and helping to guard against bloat or gastric torsion, a condition that is common in deep-chested dogs like the Fila Brasileiro. The most important thing is to buy sturdy bowls since, again, anything is in danger of being chewed by puppy teeth and you do not want your dog to be constantly chewing apart his bowl (for his safety and for your wallet!).

CLEANING SUPPLIES
Until a pup is house-trained, you will be doing a lot of cleaning. Accidents will occur, which

Note the thickness of the chain collar used on this adult Fila. Be sure that you put your Fila's collar on properly. It should be snug, but not too tight or loose.

CHOOSE THE PROPER COLLAR

The BUCKLE COLLAR is the standard collar used for everyday purposes. Be sure that you adjust the buckle on growing puppies. Check it every day. It can become too tight overnight! These collars can be made of leather or nylon. Attach your dog's identification tags to this collar.

The CHOKE CHAIN is the usual collar recommended for training. It is constructed of highly polished steel so that it slides easily through the stainless steel loop. The idea is that the dog controls the pressure around his neck and he will stop pulling if the collar becomes uncomfortable. Never leave a choke collar on your dog when not training.

The HALTER is for a trained dog that has to be restrained to prevent running away, chasing a cat and the like. Considered the most humane of all collars, it is frequently used on smaller dogs for which collars are not comfortable.

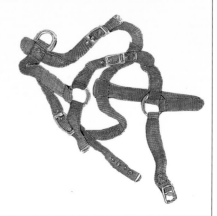

Provide your Fila Brasileiro with food and water bowls. These bowls can be constructed of sturdy plastic, ceramic, clay or stainless steel. The stainless steel ones are most dependable, durable and sanitary.

is okay for now because the puppy does not know any better. All you can do is clean up any accidents—old rags, towels, newspapers and a safe disinfectant are good to have on hand.

BEYOND THE BASICS

The items previously discussed are the bare necessities. You will find out what else you need as you go along—grooming supplies, flea/tick protection,

etc.—these things will vary depending on your situation. It is important that from the beginning you have everything you need to feed and make your Fila Brasileiro comfortable in his first few days at home.

PUPPY-PROOFING YOUR HOME

Aside from making sure that your Fila Brasileiro will be comfortable in your home, you also have to make sure that your home is safe for your Fila Brasileiro. This means taking

PHOTO COURTESY OF MIKKI PET PRODUCTS.

precautions to make sure that your pup will not get into anything he should not get into and that there is nothing within his reach that may harm him should he sniff it, chew it, inspect it, etc. This probably seems obvious since, while you are primarily concerned with your pup's safety, at the same time you do not want your belongings to be ruined. If the dog is to be limited to certain places within the house, keep any potentially dangerous items in the "off-limits" areas. An electrical cord can pose a danger should the puppy decide to taste it—and who is going to convince a pup that it would not make a great chew toy? Cords should be fastened tightly against the wall. If your dog is going to spend time in a crate, make sure that there is nothing near his crate that he can reach if he sticks his curious little nose or paws through the openings. Just as you would with a child, keep all household cleaners and chemicals where the pup cannot get to them.

It is just as important to make sure that the outside of your home is safe. Your puppy should never be unsupervised, but a pup let loose in the yard will want to run and explore, and he should be granted that freedom. Do not let a fence give you a false sense of security;

you would be surprised how crafty (and persistent) a dog can be in figuring out how to dig under or to jump or climb over a fence. The remedy is to make the fence high enough so that it is impossible for your dog to get over it (about 8 feet) and well embedded into the ground. Be sure to repair or secure any gaps in the fence. Check the fence periodically to ensure that it is in good shape and make repairs as needed; a very determined pup may return to the same spot to "work on it" until he is able to get through.

FIRST TRIP TO THE VET

Now you have picked out your puppy, your home and family are ready, all you have to do is

Responsible, law-abiding dog owners pick up their dogs' droppings whenever they are in public. Pooper-scooper devices make the job quick and easy.

collect your Fila Brasileiro from the breeder and the fun begins, right? Well...not so fast. Something else you need to prepare is your pup's first trip to the veterinarian. Perhaps the breeder can recommend someone in the area who has a good reputation with large dogs or maybe you know some other Fila owners who can suggest a

CHEMICAL TOXINS
Scour your carport for potential puppy dangers. Remove weed killers, pesticides and antifreeze materials. Antifreeze is highly toxic and even a few drops can kill an adult dog. The sweet taste attracts the animal, who will quickly consume it from the floor or curbside.

This 15-month-old Fila has a sizeable yard with high fencing to keep him securely on his owner's well-protected property.

good vet. Either way, you should have an appointment arranged for your pup in advance; plan on taking him for a checkup within the first few days of bringing him home.

The pup's first visit will consist of an overall examination to make sure that the pup does not have any problems that are not apparent to you. The veterinarian will also set up a schedule for the pup's vaccinations; the breeder will inform you of which ones the pup has already received and the vet can continue from there.

INTRODUCTION TO THE FAMILY

Everyone in the house will be excited about the puppy's coming home and will want to pet him and play with him, but it is best to make the introductions low-key so as not to overwhelm the puppy. He is apprehensive already; it is the first time he has been separated from his dam and the breeder, and the ride to your home is likely the first time he has been in a car. The last thing you want to do is smother him, as this will only frighten him further. This is not to say that human contact is not extremely necessary at this stage, because this is the time when an instant connection between the pup and his human family is formed. Gentle petting and soothing words should help console him, as well as just putting him down and letting him explore on his own (under your watchful eye, of course).

The pup may approach the family members or may busy himself with exploring for awhile. Gradually, each person should spend some time with the pup, one at a time, crouching down to get as close to the pup's level as possible and letting him sniff their hands and petting him gently. He definitely needs human attention and he needs to be touched—this is

NATURAL TOXINS

Examine your grass and landscaping before bringing your puppy home. Many varieties of plants have leaves, stems or flowers that are toxic if ingested, and you can depend on a curious puppy to investigate them. Ask your vet for information on poisonous plants or research them at your library.

If you see your dog carrying a piece of vegetation in his mouth, approach him in a quiet, disinterested manner, avoid eye contact, pet him and gradually remove the plant from his mouth. Alternatively, offer him a treat and maybe he'll drop the plant on his own accord. Be sure no toxic plants are growing in your own yard or kept in your home.

how to form an immediate bond. Just remember that the pup is experiencing a lot of things for the first time, all at the same time. There are new people, new noises, new smells and new things to investigate, so be gentle, be affectionate and be as comforting as you can be.

YOUR PUP'S FIRST NIGHT HOME

You have traveled home with your new charge safely in his crate. He has been to the vet for a thorough checkup, he has been weighed, his papers examined, perhaps he has even been vaccinated and wormed. He has met the family and has explored his area, his new bed, the yard and anywhere else he has been permitted. He has eaten his first

BOY OR GIRL?

An important consideration to be discussed is the sex of your puppy. For a family companion, a bitch may be the better choice, considering the female's inbred concern for all young creatures and her accompanying tolerance and patience. It is always advisable to spay a pet bitch, which may guarantee her a longer life.

meal at home and relieved himself in the proper place. He has heard lots of new sounds, smelled new friends and seen more of the outside world than ever before.

That was just the first day! He is worn out and is ready for bed...or so you think!

It is puppy's first night and you are ready to say "Good night"—keep in mind that this is puppy's first night to be sleeping alone. His dam and littermates are no longer at paw's length and he is a bit scared, cold and lonely. Be reassuring to your new family member. This is not the time to spoil him and give in to his inevitable whining.

Puppies whine. They whine to let the others know where they are and hopefully to find company. Place your pup in his new bed or crate in his room and close the door. Mercifully, he will fall asleep without a peep. When the inevitable occurs, ignore the whining; he is fine. Be strong and keep his interest in mind. Do not allow your heart to become guilty and visit the pup. He will fall asleep.

Many breeders recommend placing a piece of bedding from his former homestead in his new bed so that he recognizes the scent of his littermates. Others still advise placing a hot water bottle in his bed for warmth. This latter may be a good idea provided the pup does not attempt to suckle—he will get good and wet and may not fall asleep so fast.

Puppy's first night can be somewhat stressful for the pup and his new family. Remember that you are setting the tone of nighttime at your house. Unless you want to play with your pup every night at 10 p.m., midnight and 2 a.m., do not initiate the habit. Your family will thank you, and so will your pup!

PREVENTING PUPPY PROBLEMS

SOCIALIZATION

Besides getting to know his new family, your puppy should be exposed to other people, animals and situations, but of course, he must not come into close contact with dogs you don't know well until his course of injections is fully complete. This will help him become well adjusted as he grows up and will help teach him how to behave in public. Your pup's socialization began at the breeder's, now it is your respon-sibility to continue. The social-ization he receives up until the age of 12 weeks is the most crit-ical, as this is the time when he forms his impressions of the outside world. Be careful during

Make the Fila pup feel comfortable and safe in his new surroundings. Do not overwhelm the pup on his first night.

the eight-to-ten-week period, also known as the fear period. The interaction he receives during this time should be gentle and reassuring. Lack of socialization can manifest itself in fear and aggression as the dog grows up. He needs lots of

RESPONSIBILITY . . .
Grooming tools, collars, leashes, dog beds and, of course, toys will be an expense to you when you first obtain your pup, and the cost will trickle on throughout your dog's lifetime. If your puppy damages or destroys your possessions (as most puppies surely will!) or something belonging to a neighbor, you can calculate additional expense. There is also flea and pest control, which every dog owner faces more than once. You must be able to handle the financial responsibility of owning a dog.

PUP MEETS WORLD
Thorough socialization includes not only meeting new people but also being introduced to new experiences such as riding in the car, having his coat brushed, hearing the television, walking in a crowd—the list is endless. The more your pup experiences, and the more positive the experiences are, the less of a shock and the less frightening it will be for your pup to encounter new things.

human contact, affection and handling from his family and exposure to other animals.

Once your pup has received his necessary vaccinations, feel free to take him out and about (on his lead, of course). Take him around the neighborhood, take him on your daily errands, let him observe people, let him meet other dogs and pets, etc. Puppies do not have to try to make friends; there will be no shortage of people who will

want to introduce themselves. This poses a unique problem for Fila Brasileiro owners. People will want to pet your Fila, but your Fila will not want them to touch him. The Fila Brasileiro has a natural *ojeriza* (aversion, dislike) towards strangers—all strangers. Some Filas begin to show this aggression as early as 12 weeks, some as late as 7 months. If you have family members or close friends that you will want your Fila to be comfortable around, then your Fila needs to be socialized with these people when he is young. Once your Fila Brasileiro grows up, it will take him a long time to truly accept new people. Fila owners need to be in control of these social encounters, so do not allow strangers to grab and touch your puppy. Encourage the puppy to meet the new people, but do not force him or overwhelm him.

CONSISTENCY IN TRAINING

Dogs, being pack animals, naturally need a leader or else they try to establish dominance in their packs. When you bring a

Filas need to know that you are close by and in control. Making a positive impression on a young Fila is the only way to mold the Fila's very stubborn mind.

The bond between human master and Fila is unbreakable. The combination of the Fila's faithfulness and his inborn dislike of strangers makes this an unstoppable guard dog.

TRAINING TIP

Training your puppy takes much patience and can be frustrating at times, but you should see results from your efforts. If you have a puppy that seems untrainable, take him to a trainer or behaviorist. The dog may have a personality problem that requires the help of a professional, or perhaps you need help in learning how to train your dog.

Brasileiro pup, with his "puppy-dog" eyes, and not cave in, give the pup almost an unfair advantage in getting the upper hand! A Fila pup will definitely test the waters to see what he can and cannot get away with. Do not give in to those pleading eyes—stand your ground when it comes to disciplining the pup and make sure that all family members do the same. It will only confuse the pup when Mother tells him to get off the couch when he is used to sitting up there with Father to watch the nightly news. Avoid discrepancies by having all members of the household decide on the rules before the pup even comes home...and be consistent in enforcing them! Early training shapes the dog's personality, so you cannot be unclear in what you expect.

dog into your family, who becomes the leader and who becomes the "pack" are entirely up to you. You need to establish yourself as the "Alpha" early on, and constantly reinforce this with your Fila puppy. Your pup's intuitive quest for dominance, coupled with the fact that it is nearly impossible to look at an adorable Fila

Because Filas are so suspicious of strangers, it is not difficult to teach them to be attack dogs. Filas are extensively used for guarding people and property.

Spending time with the growing Fila intensifies the bond between dog and owner. This owner and his Fila pup are taking a break from training for a drink.

COMMON PUPPY PROBLEMS

The best way to prevent problems is to be proactive in stopping an undesirable behavior as soon as it starts. The old saying "You can't teach an old dog new tricks" does not necessarily hold true, but it is true that it is much easier to discourage bad behavior in a young developing pup than to wait until the pup's bad behavior becomes the adult dog's bad habit. There are some problems that are especially prevalent in puppies as they develop.

NIPPING

As puppies start to teethe, they feel the need to sink their teeth into anything...unfortunately that includes your fingers, arms, hair, toes...whatever happens to be available. You may find this behavior cute for about the first five seconds...until you feel just how sharp those puppy teeth are. This is something you want to discourage immediately and consistently with a firm "No!" (or whatever number of firm "Nos" it takes for him to under-

NO CHOCOLATE!

Use treats to bribe your dog into a desired behavior. Try small pieces of hard cheese or freeze-dried liver. Never offer chocolate as it has toxic qualities for dogs.

The dam chews on a toy while her puppy chews on his mother's ear! The mother-puppy bond is what your pup is missing when you take him home. That's what makes him cry the first night in your home, so you must reassure him and put him at ease.

stand that you mean business) and then replace your finger with an appropriate chew toy. While this behavior is merely annoying when the dog is still young, it will become dangerous as your Fila Brasileiro's adult teeth grow in and his jaws

CHEWING TIPS

Chewing goes hand in hand with nipping in the sense that a teething puppy is always looking for a way to soothe his aching gums. In this case, instead of chewing on you, he may have taken a liking to your favorite shoe or something else that he should not be chewing. Again, realize that this is a normal canine behavior that does not need to be discouraged, only redirected. Your pup just needs to be taught what is acceptable to chew on and what is off-limits. Consistently tell him "No!" when you catch him chewing on something forbidden and give him a chew toy.

Conversely, praise him when you catch him chewing on something appropriate. In this way, you are discouraging the inappropriate behavior and reinforcing the desired behavior. The puppy's chewing should stop after his adult teeth have come in, but an adult dog continues to chew for various reasons—perhaps because he is bored, needs to relieve tension or just likes to chew. That is why it is important to redirect his chewing when he is still young.

develop if he thinks that it is okay to gnaw on human appendages. You do not want to take a chance with a Fila Brasileiro; this is a breed whose jaws become large and very strong. He may not mean any harm with a friendly nip, but he also does not know his own strength.

CRYING

Your pup will sometimes cry, whine, whimper, howl or make some type of commotion when he is left alone. This is basically his way of calling out for attention, of calling out to make sure that you know he is there and that you have not forgotten about him. He may feel insecure when he is left alone, for example, when you are out of the house and he is in his crate or when you are in another part of the house and he cannot see you. The noise he is making is an expression of the anxiety he feels at being alone, so he needs to be taught that being alone is okay. You are not actually training the dog to stop making noise, you are training him to feel comfortable when he is alone and thus removing the need for him to make the noise. This is where the crate with cozy bedding and a toy comes in handy. You want to know that he is safe when you are not there to supervise, and you know that he will be safe in his crate rather than roaming freely about the house. In order for the pup to stay in his crate without making a fuss, he needs to be comfortable there. It is extremely important that the crate is never used as a form of punishment, or the pup will have a negative association with the crate.

Accustom the pup to the crate in short, gradually increasing time intervals in which you put him in the crate, maybe with a treat, and stay in the room with him. If he cries or makes a fuss, do not go to him, but stay in his sight. Gradually he will realize that staying in his crate is okay without your help, and it will not be so traumatic for him when you are not around. You may want to leave the radio on softly when you leave the house; the sound of human voices may be comforting to him.

If properly socialized, Filas get along well with other animals. The Siamese cat, perhaps not entirely convinced of the Fila's affection, is not about to test the waters.

FILA BRASILEIRO

DIETARY AND FEEDING CONSIDERATIONS

Today the choices of food for your Fila Brasileiro are many and varied. There are simply dozens of brands of food in all sorts of flavors and textures, ranging from puppy diets to those for seniors. There are even hypoallergenic and low-calorie diets available. Because your Fila's food has a bearing on coat, health and temperament, it is essential that the most suitable diet is selected for a Fila of his age. It is fair to say, however, that even dedicated owners can be somewhat perplexed by the enormous range of foods available. Only understanding what is best for your dog will help you reach a valued decision.

Dog foods are produced in three basic types: dry, semi-moist and canned. Dry foods are useful for the cost-conscious for overall they tend to be less expensive than semi-moist or canned. These contain the least fat and the most preservatives. In general, canned foods are made up of 60–70% water, while semi-moist ones often contain so much sugar that they are perhaps the least preferred by owners, even though their dogs seem to like them.

When selecting your dog's diet, three stages of development must be considered: the puppy stage, the adult stage and the senior stage.

FOOD PREFERENCE

Selecting the best dry dog food is difficult. There is no majority consensus among veterinary scientists as to the value of nutrient analysis (protein, fat, fiber, moisture, ash, cholesterol, minerals, etc.). All agree that feeding trials are what matter most, but you also have to consider the individual dog. The dog's weight, age and activity level, and what pleases his taste, all must be considered. It is probably best to take the advice of your veterinarian. Every dog has individual dietary requirements, and should be fed accordingly.

If your dog is fed a good dry food, he does not require supplements of meat or vegetables. Dogs do appreciate a little variety in their diets, so you may choose to stay with the same brand but vary the flavor. Alternatively, you may wish to add a little flavored stock to give a difference to the taste.

PUPPY STAGE

Puppies have a natural instinct to suck milk from their mother's breasts. They should exhibit this behavior the first day of their lives. If they do not suckle within a few hours, you should attempt to put them onto their mother's nipple. Their failure to feed means that you have to feed them yourself under the advice and guidance of a veterinarian. This will involve a baby bottle and a special formula. Their mother's milk is much better than any formula because it contains colostrum, a sort of antibiotic milk that protects the puppy during the first eight to ten weeks of their lives.

Puppies should be allowed to nurse for six weeks and they should be slowly weaned away from their mother by introducing small portions of meat and other solid foods after they are about one month old.

By the time they are eight weeks old, they should be completely weaned and fed a puppy dry food. During this weaning period, the diet is most important as the puppy grows fastest during his first year of life. Many Fila owners choose to feed a natural diet, which combines a high-quality dry food with cooked meat, rice and vegetables. Speak to the breeder to find out what they were feeding the puppies. You can also have your veterinarian recommend a quality growth diet for your puppy.

Though your Fila puppy should be eating a balanced diet, you may still want to talk to your veterinarian about vitamins or other supplements. Many Fila Brasileiro owners give their dogs vitamin C, starting when they are puppies. It is believed that taking vitamin C helps prevent canine hip dysplasia, a common

---

FEEDING TIPS

- Dog food must be served at room temperature, neither too hot nor too cold. Fresh water, changed often and served in a clean bowl, is mandatory, especially when feeding dry food.
- Never feed your dog from the table while you are eating, and never feed your dog leftovers from your own meal. They usually contain too much fat and too much seasoning.
- Dogs must chew their food. Hard pellets are excellent; soups and stews are to be avoided.
- Don't add leftovers or any extras to commercial dog food. The normal food is usually balanced, and adding something extra destroys the balance.
- Except for age-related changes, dogs do not require dietary variations. They can be fed the same diet, day after day, without their becoming bored or ill.

problem in the Fila Brasileiro. You can talk to your breeder about any other supplements that he gives his pups. Do not initiate any supplementation without discussing it with your breeder.

As important as what your puppy eats, is how he eats. You do not want to feed your puppy one giant meal. Split his food up into three smaller feedings. Feeding your dog smaller meals, rather than one large one, helps prevent bloat, or gastric torsion, which is more common in deep-chested dogs. When your puppy reaches six months of age, you can feed him two meals a day from then on.

ADULT DIETS

A dog is considered an adult when he has stopped growing, so in general the diet of a Fila can be changed to an adult one at about 10 to 12 months of age. The growth is in height and/or length. Do not consider the dog's weight when the decision is

made to switch from a puppy diet to a maintenance diet. Because the Fila Brasileiro is such a large dog, some people recommend switching your Fila puppy to an adult-maintenance diet early (sometimes as early as six months) to slow the rate of growth. Again you should rely upon your veterinarian and/or breeder to recommend an acceptable maintenance diet, and to let you know when to start your pup on this diet. Major dog-food manufacturers specialize in this type of food and it is just necessary for you to select the one best suited to your dog's needs. Active dogs have different nutritional requirements than sedate dogs.

A Fila Brasileiro reaches adulthood at about two years of age, though some dogs fully mature at 18 months, while others may take up to three years.

SENIOR DIETS

As dogs get older, their metabolism changes. The older dog usually exercises less, moves more slowly and sleeps more. This change in lifestyle and physiological performance requires a change in diet. Since these changes take place slowly, they might not be recognizable. What is easily recognizable is weight gain. If you continue to feed your dog an adult-mainte-

TEST FOR PROPER DIET

A good test for proper diet is the color, odor and firmness of your dog's stool. A healthy dog usually produces three semi-hard stools per day. The stools should have no unpleasant odor. They should be the same color from excretion to excretion.

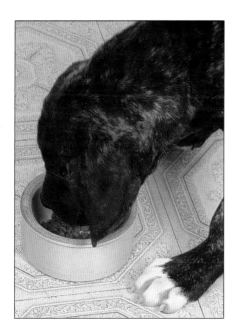

rice. Be sensitive to your senior Fila Brasileiro's diet and this will help control other problems that may arise with your old friend.

WATER

Just as your dog needs proper nutrition from his food, water is an essential "nutrient" as well. Water keeps the dog's body properly hydrated and promotes normal function of the body's systems. During housebreaking, it is necessary to keep an eye on how much water your Fila Brasileiro is drinking, but once he is reliably trained he should have access to clean fresh water at all times except meal times. Make sure that the dog's water bowl is clean, and change the

Your breeder should be able to advise you on the amount and brand of food on which to start your Fila puppy.

nance diet when he is slowing down metabolically, your dog will gain weight. Obesity in an older dog compounds the health problems that frequently accompany old age.

As dogs gets older, few of their organs function up to par. The kidneys slow down and the intestines become less efficient. These age-related factors are best handled with a change in diet and a change in feeding schedule to give smaller portions that are more easily digested.

There is no single best diet for every older dog. While many dogs do well on light or senior diets, other dogs do better on puppy diets or other special premium diets such as lamb and

GRAIN-BASED DIETS

Some less expensive dog foods are based on grains and other plant proteins. While these products may appear to be attractively priced, most breeders prefer a diet based on animal proteins and believe that they are more conducive to your dog's health. Many grain-based diets rely on soy protein, which may cause flatulence (passing gas).

There are many cases, however, when your dog might require a special diet. These special requirements should only be recommended by your veterinarian.

This handsome Fila
is taking a much
needed water
break after a
morning of play
with his master.
For such large
dogs, Filas require
considerable
exercise.

to provide your dog with the exercise he needs. Regular walks, play sessions in the yard or letting the dog run free in the yard under your supervision are all sufficient forms of exercise for the Fila Brasileiro. For those who are more ambitious, you will find that your Fila Brasileiro will be able to keep up with you on extra long walks or the morning run. However, make sure not to run with your Fila until he is eight or nine months old to help prevent problems with his hips and other joints.

water often, making sure that water is always available for your dog.

EXERCISE

All dogs require some form of exercise, regardless of breed. A sedentary lifestyle is as harmful to a dog as it is to a person. The Fila Brasileiro happens to be an active breed that needs a considerable amount of exercise, but you do not have to be a weightlifter or marathon runner

Not only is exercise essential for his physical fitness, it is essential to his mental well-being. A bored dog will find something to do, which often manifests itself in some type of destructive behavior. In this sense, it is essential for the owner's mental well-being as well!

A Worthy Investment

Veterinary studies have proven that a balanced high-quality diet pays off in your dog's coat quality, behavior and activity level. Invest in premium brands for the maximum payoff with your dog.

Fortunately the Fila has an easy-care coat that requires minimal brushing and only occasional bathing. It naturally keeps its sheen and healthy appearance.

GROOMING

BRUSHING

A natural bristle brush or a slicker brush can be used for regular routine brushing. Brushing is effective for removing dead hair and stimulating the dog's natural oils to add shine and a healthy look to the coat. Your Fila Brasileiro is not a breed that needs excessive grooming, but his smooth coat should be brushed weekly as part of routine maintenance. Routine brushing will get rid of dust and dandruff and remove any dead hair. Regular grooming sessions are also a good way to spend time with your dog. Many dogs grow to like the feel of being brushed and will enjoy the routine.

BATHING

Dogs do not need to be bathed as often as humans, but sometimes bathing is necessary. Again, like most anything, if you accustom your pup to being bathed as a puppy, it will be second nature by the time he grows up. You want your dog to be at ease in the bath or else it could end up a wet, soapy, messy ordeal for both of you!

Brush your Fila Brasileiro thoroughly before wetting his coat. This will get rid of dust and dead hair. Make sure that your dog is standing on a good non-slip surface. Begin by wetting the dog's coat. A shower or hose attachment is necessary for thoroughly wetting and rinsing the coat. Check the water temperature to make sure that it is neither too hot nor too cold.

Next, apply shampoo to the dog's coat and work it into a good lather. You should purchase a shampoo that is

GROOMING EQUIPMENT

How much grooming equipment you purchase will depend on how much grooming you are going to do. Here are some basics:

- Pin brush
- Metal comb
- Scissors
- Rubber mat
- Dog shampoo
- Spray hose attachment
- Towels
- Blow dryer
- Ear cleaner
- Cotton balls
- Nail clippers
- Dental care products

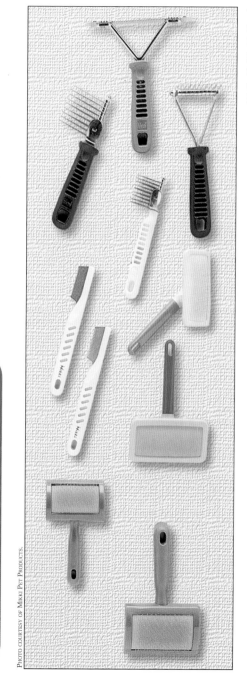

Your local pet shop will have a large supply of grooming tools that you can use on your Fila Brasileiro.

PHOTO COURTESY OF MIKKI PET PRODUCTS.

In these unique scanning electron micrographs (SEMS), presented here for the first time, are the hairs of a healthy Fila. This photo shows a Fila hair root enlarged 150 times. The facing page shows three hairs of different thicknesses, which cover the dog's body. The enlargement is 175 times natural size. These images were prepared especially for this book by Dr. Dennis Kunkel from the University of Hawaii.

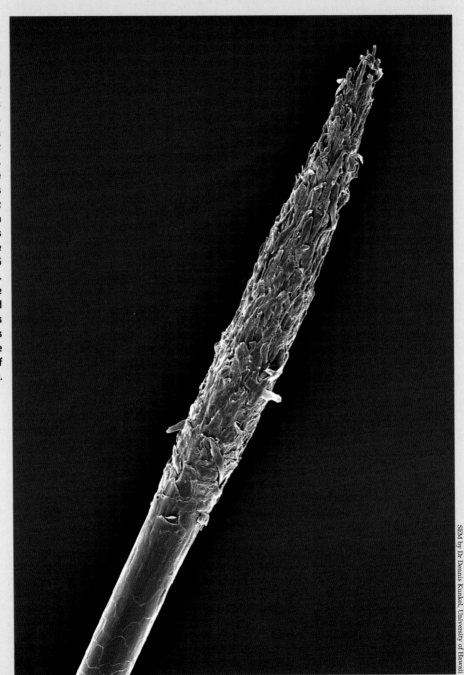

SEM by Dr Dennis Kunkel, University of Hawaii

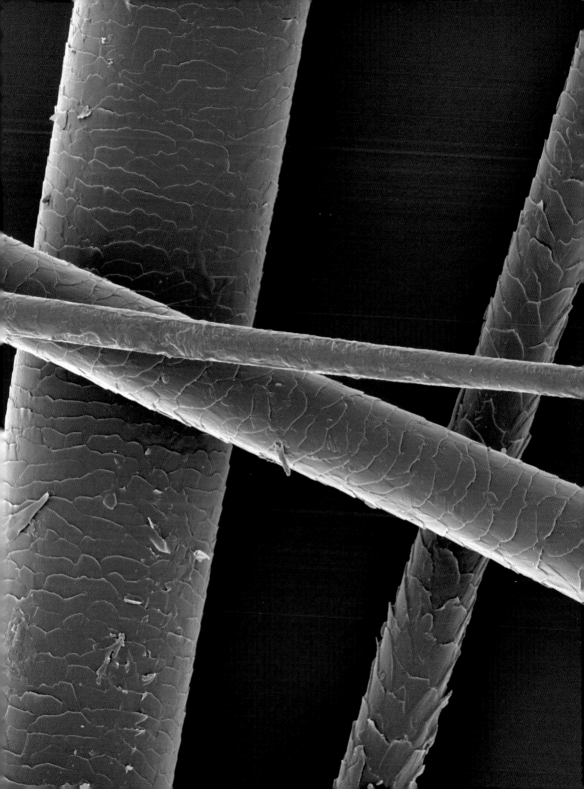

Be very careful in cleaning your Fila's ears. Inspect the ear for the presence of mites while doing the cleaning.

The nails of a Fila puppy are sharp, small and easily cut. It is advisable to train the puppy to tolerate nail clipping while he's still a puppy.

your dog to shake out his coat—you might want to stand back, but make sure you have a hold on the dog to keep him from running through the house.

EAR CLEANING

Breeds with pendulous ears, like the Fila Brasileiro, are more prone to ear infections. The ears should be kept clean at all times. Ears can be cleaned with a cotton ball and special cleaner or ear powder made especially for dogs. Be on the lookout for any signs of infection or ear-mite infestation. If your Fila Brasileiro shakes his head or scratches at his ears frequently, this usually indicates an ear mite problem. If his ears have an unusual odor, this is also a sign of mite infestation or infection, and a signal to have his ears checked by the veterinarian.

made for dogs; do not use a product made for human hair. Wash the head last; you do not want shampoo to drip into the dog's eyes while you are washing the rest of his body. Work the shampoo all the way down to the skin. You can use this opportunity to check the skin for any bumps, bites or other abnormalities. Do not neglect any area of the body—get all of the hard-to-reach places.

Once the dog has been thoroughly shampooed, he requires an equally thorough rinsing. Shampoo left in the coat can be irritating to the skin. Protect his eyes from the shampoo by shielding them with your hand and directing the flow of water in the opposite direction. You should also avoid getting water in the ear canal. Be prepared for

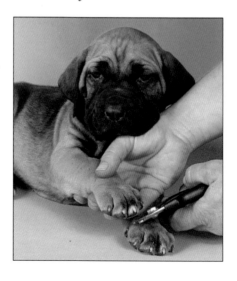

NAIL CLIPPING

Your Fila Brasileiro should be accustomed to having his nails trimmed at an early age, since it will be part of your maintenance routine throughout his life. Keeping the nails short is not just a cosmetic consideration, but a safety precaution in a dog as powerful as a Fila, preventing an unintentional scratch should the dog attempt to jump up. A long nail has a better chance of ripping and bleeding, or causing the feet to spread. A good rule of thumb is that if you can hear your dog's nails clicking on the floor when he walks, his nails are too long.

Before you start cutting, make sure you can identify the "quick" in each nail. The quick is a blood vessel that runs through the center of each nail and grows rather close to the end. It will bleed if accidentally cut, which will be quite painful for the dog as it contains nerve endings. Keep some type of clotting agent on hand, such as a styptic pencil or styptic powder (the type used for shaving). This will stop the bleeding quickly when applied to the end of the cut nail. Do not panic if you cut the quick, just stop the bleeding and talk soothingly to your dog. Once he has calmed down, move on to the next nail. It is better to clip a little at a time, particularly with black-nailed dogs. (If

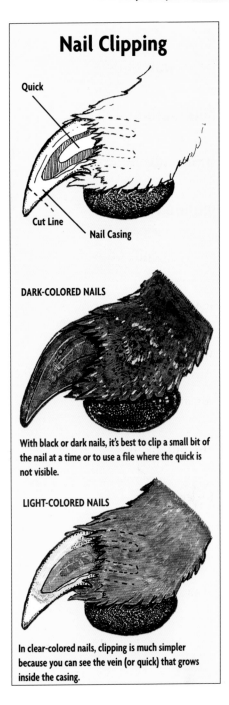

Nail Clipping

Quick

Cut Line

Nail Casing

DARK-COLORED NAILS

With black or dark nails, it's best to clip a small bit of the nail at a time or to use a file where the quick is not visible.

LIGHT-COLORED NAILS

In clear-colored nails, clipping is much simpler because you can see the vein (or quick) that grows inside the casing.

PEDICURE TIP

A dog that spends a lot of time outside on a hard surface, such as cement or pavement, will have his nails naturally worn down and may not need to have them trimmed as often. It is best to get your dog accustomed to the nail-trimming procedure at an early age so that he is used to it. Some dogs are especially sensitive about having their feet touched, but if a dog has experienced it since puppyhood, it should not bother him.

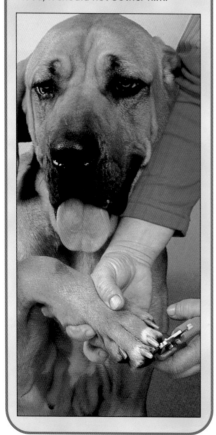

you have a hard time trying to identify how much to clip, you may want to have your veterinarian show you the correct way to clip the nails.)

Hold your pup steady as you begin trimming his nails; you do not want him to make any sudden movements or run away. Talk to him soothingly and stroke him as you clip. Holding his foot in your hand, simply take off the end of each nail in one quick clip. You can purchase nail clippers that are specially made for dogs; you can probably find them wherever you buy pet supplies.

TRAVELING WITH YOUR DOG

CAR TRAVEL

You should accustom your Fila Brasileiro to riding in a car at an early age. You may or may not often take him in the car, but, at the very least, he will need to go to the vet and you do not want these trips to be traumatic for the dog or a big hassle for you. Keep in mind that you will not fit a full-grown Fila Brasileiro in your compact car! You will need a large car or utility vehicle to accommodate a 150-lb Fila in his king-sized crate!

Put the pup in the crate and see how he reacts. If he seems uneasy, you can have a passenger hold him on his lap while you drive. However, this will not work with an adult Fila, so be sure to acclimate him to his crate (immediately) before he gets too big. Another option is a specially made safety harness for dogs, which straps the dog in much like a seat belt. This is an excellent choice if your vehicle will not fit the dog's crate. Never let the Fila loose in the vehicle—this is very dangerous! If you should stop short, your dog can be thrown and injured. It is an unsafe situation for everyone—human and canine.

For long trips, be prepared to stop to let the dog relieve himself. Bring along whatever you need to clean up after him. You should take along some paper kitchen towels and perhaps some old bath towels for use should he have an accident in the car or suffer from motion sickness.

Air Travel

Contact your chosen airline before proceeding with your travel plans that include your Fila. The dog will be required to travel in a fiberglass crate and you should always check in advance with the airline regarding specific requirements for the crate's size, type and labeling. To help put the dog at ease, give him one of his favorite toys in the crate. Do not feed the dog for several hours prior to checking in so that you minimize his need to relieve himself.

However, some airlines require that the dog must be fed within four hours of arriving at the airport, in which case a light meal is best.

Make sure your dog is properly identified and that your contact information appears on his ID tags and on his crate. Your Fila will travel in a different area

Traveling by car with a Fila is never a simple matter. Most cars are too small to accommodate a Fila in his crate, so a larger sport-utility vehicle is needed. It is not advisable to travel with a Fila loose in a car.

TRAVEL TIP
However much your dog enjoys traveling, he should never be left alone in a car in warm weather, even with the windows left open. Heat builds up all too quickly and can cause suffering and tragedy. Even on a cloudy day one must always be aware that the sun can break through unexpectedly.

dogs the size of a Fila Brasileiro. Also, you do not want to reserve a place for your family without mentioning that you are bringing along a dog...a big dog...because if it is against their policy you may not have a place to stay.

Alternatively, if you are traveling and choose not to take your Fila Brasileiro, you will have to make arrangements for him while you are away. Because of the Fila's aversion towards strangers, a boarding kennel will probably not be a viable option. You may want to have a family member, friend or neighbor stay at your house or keep your Fila at their home. This will have to be someone your Fila Brasileiro knows and trusts. If you are someone who travels a lot and cannot take your Fila with you, you may want to consider another breed. This is not a dog you can just drop off anywhere or have strangers come in to feed. It will require planning ahead on your

Select a boarding kennel convenient to your home. The kennel should be neat, clean and spacious, and have a program that will enable your dog to be exercised properly.

of the plane than the human passengers, so every rule must be strictly followed to prevent the risk of getting separated from your dog.

VACATION PLANS

So you want to take a family vacation—and you want to include *all* members of the family. You would probably make arrangements for accommodations ahead of time anyway, but this is especially important when traveling with a dog—a *big* dog. You do not want to make an overnight stop at the only place around for miles to find out that they do not allow dogs, or do not allow

ON THE ROAD

If you are going on a long motor trip with your dog, be sure the hotels are dog-friendly. Many hotels do not accept dogs. Also take along some ice that can be thawed and offered to your dog if he becomes overheated. Most dogs like to lick ice.

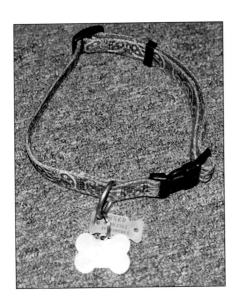

part to make sure you have a reliable "babysitter" for your Fila.

IDENTIFICATION

Your Fila Brasileiro is your valued companion and friend. That is why you always keep a close eye on him and you have made sure that he cannot escape from the yard or break out of his collar and run away from you. However, accidents can happen and there may come a time when your dog unexpectedly gets separated from you. If this unfortunate event should occur, the first thing on your mind will be finding him. Proper identification will increase the chances of his being returned to you safely and quickly.

IDENTIFICATION OPTIONS

As puppies become more and more expensive, especially those puppies of high quality for showing and/or breeding, they have a greater chance of being stolen. The usual collar dog tag is, of course, easily removed. But there are two more permanent techniques that have become widely used for identification.

The puppy microchip implantation involves the injection of a small microchip, about the size of a corn kernel, under the skin of the dog. If your dog shows up at a clinic or shelter, or is offered for resale under less-than-savory circumstances, it can be positively identified by the microchip. The microchip is scanned, and a registry quickly identifies the owner.

Tattooing is done on various parts of the dog, from his belly to his ears. The number tattooed can be your telephone number, your dog's registration number or any other number that you can easily remember. When professional dog thieves see a tattooed dog, they usually lose interest. For the safety of our dogs, no laboratory facility or dog broker will accept a tattooed dog as stock.

Discuss microchipping and tattooing with your veterinarian and breeder. Some vets perform these services on their own premises for a reasonable fee. To ensure that your dog's identification is effective, be certain that the dog is then properly registered with a legitimate national database.

Your Fila should always be wearing a collar to which are attached proper identification tags.

TRAINING YOUR
FILA BRASILEIRO

Living with an untrained dog is a lot like owning a piano that you do not know how to play—it is a nice object to look at but it does not do much more than that to bring you pleasure. Now try taking piano lessons and suddenly the piano comes alive and brings forth magical sounds and rhythms that set your heart singing and your body swaying.

The same is true with your Fila Brasileiro. At first you enjoy seeing him around the house. He does not do much with you other than need food, water and exercise. He is a big responsibility

ATTENTION!
Your dog is actually training you at the same time you are training him. Dogs do things to get attention. They usually repeat whatever succeeds in getting your attention.

with a small return. He develops unacceptable behaviors that annoy and/or infuriate you to say nothing of bad habits that may end up costing you great sums of money.

To train your Fila Brasileiro, you may like to enroll in an

A young Fila puppy is a dry sponge, ready to soak up whatever information and guidance you give him.

obedience class. Teach him good manners as you learn how and why he behaves the way he does. Find out how to communicate with your dog and how to recognize and understand his communications with you. Suddenly the dog takes on a new role in your life—he is smart, interesting, well behaved and fun to be with. He demonstrates his bond of devotion to you daily. In other words, your Fila Brasileiro does wonders for your ego because he constantly reminds you that you are not only his leader, you are his hero! Miraculous things have happened—you have a wonderful dog (even your family and friends have noticed the transformation!) and you feel good about yourself.

Those involved with teaching dog obedience and counseling owners about their dogs' behavior have discovered some interesting facts about dog ownership. For example, training dogs when they are puppies results in the highest rate of success in developing well-mannered and well-adjusted adult dogs. Training an older dog, say from six months to six years of age, can produce almost equal results providing that the owner accepts the dog's slower rate of learning capability and is willing to work patiently to help the dog succeed at developing to his fullest potential. Unfortunately, the patience factor is what many owners of untrained adult dogs

Make your Fila puppy understand exactly what is expected of him indoors and out. A Fila puppy is most trainable before the age of six months. Take advantage of this period when the puppy craves attention and instruction.

lack, so they do not persist until their dogs are successful at learning particular behaviors.

Training a puppy, aged 10 to 16 weeks (20 weeks at the most), is like working with a dry sponge in a pool of water. The pup soaks up whatever you show him and constantly looks for more things to do and learn. At this early age,

OBEDIENCE SCHOOL

Taking your dog to an obedience school may be the best investment in time and money you can ever make. You will enjoy the benefits for the lifetime of your dog and you will have the opportunity to meet people who have similar expectations for companion dogs.

Fila puppies respond best to gentle motivation. Despite their size and power, Filas do not respond best to forceful training methods. Treat the puppy as the sensitive creature he is.

HONOR AND OBEY
Dogs are the most honorable animals in existence. They consider another species (humans) as their own. They interface with you. You are their leader. Puppies perceive children to be on their level; their actions around small children are different from their behavior around their adult masters.

his body is not yet producing hormones, and therein lies the reason for such a high rate of success. Without hormones, he is focused on his owners and not particularly interested in investigating other places, dogs, people, etc. You are his leader; his provider of food, water, shelter and security. Therefore, he latches onto you and wants to stay close. He will usually follow you from room to room, and will not let you out of his sight when you are outdoors with him.

Once the puppy begins to produce hormones, his natural curiosity emerges and he begins to investigate the world around him. It is at this time when you may notice that the untrained dog begins to wander away from you and even ignores your commands to stay close.

Occasionally there are no classes available within a reasonable distance of the owner's home but you can also do a lot to train your dog yourself. Sometimes there are classes available but the tuition is too costly. Whatever the circumstances, the solution to the problem of training your Fila without formal obedience classes lies within the pages of this book.

This chapter is devoted to helping you train your Fila Brasileiro at home. If the recommended procedures are followed faithfully, you may expect positive results that will prove

THINK BEFORE YOU BARK
Dogs are sensitive to their masters' moods and emotions. Use your voice wisely when communicating with your dog. Never raise your voice at your dog unless you are trying to correct him. "Barking" at your dog can become as meaningless as "dogspeak" is to you.

rewarding to both you and your dog.

Whether your Fila Brasileiro is a puppy or a mature adult, the methods of teaching and the techniques we use in training basic

behaviors are the same. After all, no dog, whether puppy or adult, likes harsh or inhumane methods. All creatures, however, respond favorably to gentle motivational methods and sincere praise and encouragement. Now let us get started.

HOUSEBREAKING
You can train a puppy to relieve himself wherever you choose, but this must be somewhere suitable. You should bear in mind from the outset that when your puppy is old enough to go out in public places any canine deposits must be removed at once, so you will

Most dogs are trained to relieve themselves on grass—the most common surface in most areas. Since Filas rarely live in urban settings, grass is the surface of choice.

always have to carry with you a small plastic bag or "poop-scoop."

Outdoor training includes such surfaces as grass, dirt and cement. Indoor training usually means training your dog to newspaper. When deciding on the surface and location that you will want your Fila Brasileiro to use, be sure it is going to be permanent. Training your dog to grass and then changing your mind two months later is extremely difficult for both dog and owner.

Next, choose the command you will use each and every time you want your puppy to void. "Go hurry up" and "Outside!" are examples of commands commonly used by dog owners. Get in the habit of giving the puppy your chosen relief command before you take him out. That way, when he becomes an adult, you will be able to determine if he wants to go out when you ask him. Confirmation will be signs of interest, such as wagging his tail, watching you intently, going to the door and the like.

PUPPY'S NEEDS

The Fila puppy needs to relieve himself after play periods, after each meal, after he has been sleeping and any time he indicates that he is looking for a place to urinate or defecate. The urinary and intestinal tract muscles of very young puppies are not fully developed.

TAKE THE LEAD
Do not carry your dog to his relief area. Lead him there on a leash or, better yet, encourage him to follow you to the spot. If you start carrying him to his spot, you might end up spoiling your dog, and you can't carry a Fila once he's over 10-12 weeks old!

Therefore, like human babies, puppies need to relieve themselves frequently.

Take your puppy out often—every hour for an eight-week-old, for example. The older the puppy, the less often he will need to relieve himself. Finally, as a mature healthy adult, he will require only three to five relief trips per day.

Canine Development Schedule

It is important to understand how and at what age a puppy develops into adulthood. If you are a puppy owner, consult the following Canine Development Schedule to determine the stage of development your puppy is currently experiencing. This knowledge will help you as you work with the puppy in the weeks and months ahead.

Period	Age	Characteristics
FIRST TO THIRD	**BIRTH TO SEVEN WEEKS**	Puppy needs food, sleep and warmth, and responds to simple and gentle touching. Needs mother for security and disciplining. Needs littermates for learning and interacting with other dogs. Pup learns to function within a pack and learns pack order of dominance. Begin socializing with adults and children for short periods. Begins to become aware of his environment.
FOURTH	**EIGHT TO TWELVE WEEKS**	Brain is fully developed. Needs socializing with outside world. Remove from mother and littermates. Needs to change from canine pack to human pack. Human dominance necessary. Fear period occurs between 8 and 16 weeks. Avoid fright and pain.
FIFTH	**THIRTEEN TO SIXTEEN WEEKS**	Training and formal obedience should begin. Less association with other dogs, more with people, places, situations. Period will pass easily if you remember this is pup's change-to-adolescence time. Be firm and fair. Flight instinct prominent. Permissiveness and over-disciplining can do permanent damage. Praise for good behavior.
JUVENILE	**FOUR TO EIGHT MONTHS**	Another fear period about 7 to 8 months of age. It passes quickly, but be cautious of fright and pain. Sexual maturity reached. Dominant traits established. Dog should understand sit, down, come and stay by now.

NOTE: THESE ARE APPROXIMATE TIME FRAMES. ALLOW FOR INDIVIDUAL DIFFERENCES IN PUPPIES.

Give the Fila an area of your home that he can call his own. Dogs will not soil in their sleeping or eating area, thus making housebreaking easier for owners.

HOUSING

Since the types of housing and control you provide for your puppy has a direct relationship on the success of house-training, we consider the various aspects of both before we begin training. Bringing a new puppy home and turning him loose in your house can be compared to turning a child loose in an amusement park and telling the child that the place is all his! The sheer enormity of the place would be too much for him to handle.

Instead, offer the puppy clearly defined areas where he can play, sleep, eat and live. A room of the house where the family gathers is the most obvious choice. Puppies are social animals and need to feel a part of the pack right from the start. Hearing your voice, watching you while you are

HOW MANY TIMES A DAY?

AGE	RELIEF TRIPS
To 14 weeks	10
14–22 weeks	8
22–32 weeks	6
Adulthood (dog stops growing)	4

These are estimates, of course, but they are a guide to the *minimum* number of opportunities a dog should have each day to relieve himself.

doing things and smelling you nearby are all positive reinforcers that he is now a member of your pack. Usually a family room, the kitchen or a nearby adjoining breakfast area is ideal for providing safety and security for both puppy and owner. Make sure the

CALM DOWN

Dogs will do anything for your attention. If you reward the dog when he is calm and attentive, you will develop a well-mannered dog. If, on the other hand, you greet your dog excitedly and encourage him to wrestle with you, the dog will greet you the same way and you will have a hyperactive dog on your hands.

room you choose does not have slippery floors, as this can cause problems for your Fila's growing body. If it has bare floors, you can purchase inexpensive rugs to cover the floor.

Within that room there should be a smaller area which the puppy can call his own. An alcove, a wire or fiberglass dog crate or a gated corner from which he can view the activities of his new family will be fine. The size of the area or crate is the key factor here. The area must be large enough for the puppy to lie down and stretch out, as well as to stand up without rubbing his head on the top, yet small enough so that he cannot relieve himself at one end and sleep at the other without coming into contact with his droppings. If you purchased an adult-sized crate for your Fila puppy, you can fill the excess space with boxes, removing them as he grows.

Dogs are, by nature, clean animals and will not remain close

Keep a watchful eye on your Fila puppy while he's in the yard. Puppies can be very industrious and mischievous. Always be aware of where your puppy is and what he's doing.

to their droppings unless given no other option. In those cases, they then become dirty dogs and usually remain that way for life. The designated area should be lined with a clean towel and offer one toy, no more. Do not put food or water in the crate, as eating and drinking will activate his digestive processes and ultimately defeat your purpose as well as make the puppy very uncomfortable as he attempts to "hold it."

Control

By *control*, we mean helping the puppy to create a lifestyle pattern that will be compatible to that of his human pack (*you!*). Just as we guide children to learn our way of life, we must show the puppy when it is time to play, eat, sleep, exercise and entertain himself.

A wire crate offers your Fila Brasileiro many advantages. In warmer climes, the wire crate is ideal for ventilation. Most Filas like to be able to see what's going on about them.

Your puppy should always sleep in his crate or his special area. He should also learn that, during times of household confusion and excessive human activity such as at breakfast when family members are preparing for the day, he can play by himself in safety and comfort in his designated area. Each time you leave the puppy alone, he should understand exactly where he is to stay. You can gradually increase the time he is left alone to get him used to it. Puppies are chewers. They cannot tell the difference between lamp cords, television wires, rawhide bones, shoes, table legs, etc. Chewing into a television wire, for example, can be fatal to the puppy while a shorted wire can start a fire in the house.

If the puppy chews on the arm of the chair when he is alone, you will probably discipline him angrily when you get home. Thus, he makes the association that your coming home means he is going to be punished. (He will not remember chewing up the chair and is

> **HOUSE-TRAINING TIP**
> Most of all, be consistent. Always take your dog to the same location, always use the same command and always have the dog on lead when he is in his relief area, unless a fenced-in yard is available.
>
> By following the Success Method, your puppy will be completely housebroken by the time his muscle and brain development reach maturity. Keep in mind that small breeds usually mature faster than large breeds, but all puppies should be trained by six months of age.

Opposite page: If your home needs guarding during your absence, the Fila is the best there is! A Fila frightens away intruders at sight...even a burglar alarm isn't that good.

incapable of making the association of the discipline with his naughty deed.)

Other times of excitement, such as family parties, friends' visits, etc., can be entertaining for the puppy providing he can view the activities from the security of his crate. He is not underfoot and he is not being fed all sorts of tidbits that will probably cause him stomach distress, yet he still feels a part of the fun.

SCHEDULE

A puppy should be taken to his relief area each time he is released from his designated

THE SUCCESS METHOD

Success that comes by luck is usually short-lived. Success that comes by well-thought-out proven methods is often more easily achieved and permanent. This is the Success Method. It is designed to give you, the puppy owner, a simple yet proven way to help your puppy develop clean living habits and a feeling of security in his new environment.

6 Steps to Successful Crate Training

1 Tell the puppy "Crate time!" and place him in the crate with a small treat (a piece of cheese or half of a biscuit). Let him stay in the crate for five minutes while you are in the same room. Then release him and praise lavishly. Never release him when he is fussing. Wait until he is quiet before you let him out.

2 Repeat Step 1 several times a day.

3 The next day, place the puppy in the crate as before. Let him stay there for ten minutes. Do this several times.

4 Continue building time in five-minute increments until the puppy stays in his crate for 30 minutes with you in the room. Always take him to his relief area after prolonged periods in his crate.

5 Now go back to Step 1 and let the puppy stay in his crate for five minutes, this time while you are out of the room.

6 Once again, build crate time in five-minute increments with you out of the room. When the puppy will stay willingly in his crate (he may even fall asleep!) for 30 minutes with you out of the room, he will be ready to stay in it for several hours at a time.

area, after meals, after a play session, when he first awakens in the morning (at age eight weeks, this can mean 5 a.m.!) and whenever he indicates by circling or sniffing busily that he needs to urinate or defecate. For a puppy less than ten weeks of age, a routine of taking him out every hour is necessary. As the puppy grows, he will be able to wait for longer periods of time.

Keep trips to his relief area short. Stay no more than five or six minutes and then return to the house. If he goes during that time, praise him lavishly and take him indoors immediately. If he does not, but he has an accident when

The growing Fila responds to kind and fair treatment. Once respect is earned, he treats his owner like his lord and master.

PRACTICE MAKES PERFECT!

- Have training lessons with your dog every day in several short segments—three to five times a day for a few minutes at a time is ideal.
- Do not have long practice sessions. The dog will become easily bored.
- Never practice when you are tired, ill, worried or in an otherwise negative mood. This will transmit to the dog and may have an adverse effect on his performance.

Think fun, short and above all *positive!* End each session on a high note, rather than a failed exercise, and make sure to give a lot of praise. Enjoy the training and help your dog enjoy it, too.

you go back indoors, pick him up immediately, say "No! No!" and return to his relief area. Wait a few minutes, then return to the house again. Never hit a puppy or put his face in urine or excrement when he has an accident!

Once indoors, put the puppy in his crate until you have had time to clean up his accident. Then release him to the family area and watch him more closely than before. Chances are, his accident was a result of your not picking up his signal or waiting too long before offering him the opportunity to relieve himself. Never hold a grudge against the puppy for accidents.

Let the puppy learn that going outdoors means it is time to relieve himself, not play. Once trained, he will be able to play indoors and out and still differentiate between the times for play versus the times for relief.

Help him develop regular hours for naps, being alone, playing by himself and just resting, all in his crate. Encourage him to entertain himself while you are busy with your activities. Let him learn that having you near is comforting, but it is not your main purpose in life to provide him with undivided attention.

PLAN TO PLAY

The puppy should also have regular play and exercise sessions when he is with you or a family member. Exercise for a very young puppy can consist of a short walk around the house or yard. Playing can include fetching games with a large ball or a special toy. (All puppies teethe and need soft things upon which to chew.) Remember to restrict play periods to indoors within his living area (the family room, for example) until he is completely house-trained.

At ten weeks of age, Philo do Camping is an irrepressible explorer. He even makes time to smell the roses—but watch out for the thorns!

A consistent daily schedule is the main factor in housebreaking. By enforcing regular times for the pup to eat and go out to his relief area, you set his daily routine.

Each time you put a puppy in his own area use the same command, whatever suits best. Soon, he will run to his crate or his own special area when he hears you say those words.

A successful house-training method provides safety for you,

the puppy and the home. It also provides the puppy with a feeling of security, and that helps the puppy achieve self-confidence and clean habits. Remember that one of the primary ingredients in house-training your puppy is control. Regardless of your lifestyle, there will always be occasions when you will need to have a place where your dog can stay and be happy and safe. Crate training is the answer for now and in the future.

In conclusion, a few key elements are really all you need for a successful house-training method—consistency, frequency, praise, control and supervision. By following these procedures with a normal, healthy puppy, you and the puppy will soon be past the stage of "accidents" and ready to move on to a clean and rewarding life together.

PAPER CAPER

Never line your pup's sleeping area with newspaper. Puppy litters are usually raised on newspaper and, once in your home, the puppy will immediately associate newspaper with voiding. Never put newspaper on any floor while house-training, as this will only confuse the puppy. If you are paper-training him, use paper in his designated relief area only. Finally, restrict water intake after evening meals. Offer a few licks at a time—never let a young puppy gulp water after meals.

ROLES OF DISCIPLINE, REWARD AND PUNISHMENT

Discipline, training one to act in accordance with rules, brings order to life. It is as simple as that. Without discipline, particularly in a group society, chaos reigns supreme and the group will eventually perish. Humans and canines are social animals and need some form of discipline in order to function effectively. They must procure food, protect their home base and their young and reproduce to keep the species going.

If there were no discipline in the lives of social animals, they would eventually die from starvation and/or predation by other stronger animals. In the case of domestic canines, dogs need discipline in their lives in order to understand how their pack (you and other family members) functions and how they must act in order to survive.

A large humane society in a highly populated area recently surveyed dog owners regarding their satisfaction with their relationships with their dogs. People who had trained their dogs were 75% more satisfied with their pets than those who had never trained their dogs.

Dr. Edward Thorndike, a noted psychologist, has established *Thorndike's Theory of Learning*, which states that a behavior that results in a pleasant event tends to be repeated. A behavior that results in an unpleasant event tends not to be repeated. It is this theory on which training methods are based today. For example, if you manipulate a dog to perform a specific behavior and reward him for doing it, he is likely to do it again because he enjoyed the end result.

Occasionally, punishment, a penalty for an offense, is necessary. The best type of punishment often comes from an outside source. For example, a child is told not to touch the stove because he may get burned.

FAMILY TIES

If you have other pets in the home and/or interact often with the pets of friends and other family members, your pup will respond to those pets in much the same manner as you do. It is only when you show fear of or resentment toward another animal that he will act fearful or unfriendly.

He disobeys and touches the stove. In doing so, he is burnt. From that time on, he respects the stove and avoids contact with it. Therefore, a behavior that results in an unpleasant event tends not to be repeated.

A good example of a dog learning the hard way is the dog who chases the house cat. He is told many times to leave the cat alone, yet he persists in teasing the cat. Then, one day he begins chasing the cat but the cat turns and swipes a claw across the dog's face, leaving him with a painful gash on his nose. The dog stops chasing the cat.

TRAINING EQUIPMENT

COLLAR

A simple buckle collar is fine for puppies and some dogs. Because of the abundance of loose skin

The Fila's collar and leash must be attached to a strong, capable arm. No matter how well trained, the Fila requires an adult handler.

around the Fila's neck and the sheer strength of these dogs, most Fila owners will find it necessary to use a chain choker collar or a pinch (or prong) collar. You must be instructed in the proper use of such equipment.

LEAD

A 6-foot lead is recommended, preferably made of leather or nylon. A chain lead is not recommended, as many dog owners find that the chain cuts into their hands and that switch-

THE CLEAN LIFE

By providing sleeping and resting quarters that fit the dog, and offering frequent opportunities to relieve himself outside his quarters, the puppy quickly learns that the outdoors is the place to go when he needs to urinate or defecate. It also reinforces his innate desire to keep his sleeping quarters clean. This, in turn, helps develop the muscle control that will eventually produce a dog with clean living habits.

Don't be afraid to use treats as motivators in training. They work well when teaching new commands, but you will eventually wean your Fila from constant food rewards.

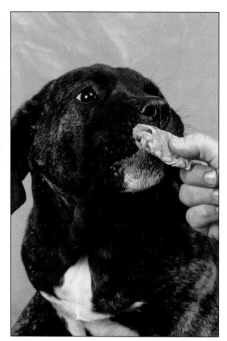

TRAINING BEGINS: ASK THE DOG A QUESTION

In order to teach your dog anything, you must first get his attention. After all, he cannot learn anything if he is looking away from you with his mind on something else.

To get his attention, say, "School?" and immediately walk over to him and give him a treat as you tell him "Good dog." Wait a minute or two and repeat the routine, this time with a treat in your hand as you approach within a foot of the dog. Hold out the treat as you ask, "School?" He will see you approaching with a treat in your hand and most likely begin walking toward you. As you meet, give him the treat and praise again.

The third time, ask the question, have a treat in your hand and walk only a short distance toward the dog so that he must walk almost all the way to you.

ing the lead back and forth frequently between their hands is painful.

TREATS

Have a bag of treats on hand. Something nutritious and easy to swallow works best; use a soft treat, a chunk of cheese or a piece of cooked chicken rather than a dry biscuit. Using food rewards will not teach a dog to beg at the table—the only way to teach a dog to beg at the table is to give him food from the table. In training, rewarding the dog with a food treat away from the table will help him associate praise and the treats with learning new behaviors that obviously please his owner.

REAP THE REWARDS

If you start with a normal, healthy dog and give him time, patience and some carefully executed lessons, you will reap the rewards of that training for the life of the dog. And what a life it will be! The two of you will find immeasurable pleasure in the companionship you have built together with love, respect and understanding.

As he reaches you, give him the treat and praise again.

By this time, the dog will probably be getting the idea that if he pays attention to you, especially when you ask that question, it will pay off in treats and fun activities for him. In other words, he learns that "school" means doing fun things with you that result in treats and positive attention for him.

Remember that the dog does not understand your verbal language, he only recognizes sounds. Your question translates to a series of sounds for him, and those sounds become the signal to go to you and pay attention; if he does, he will get to interact with you plus receive treats and praise.

LANGUAGE BARRIER

Dogs do not understand our language and have to rely on tone of voice more than just words or sound. They can be trained to react to a certain sound, at a certain volume. If you say "No, Oliver" in a very soft, pleasant voice, it will not have the same meaning as "No, Oliver!!" when you raise your voice.

You should never use the dog's name during a reprimand, just the command "No! " You never want the dog to associate his name with a negative experience or reprimand.

THE BASIC COMMANDS

TEACHING SIT

Now that you have the dog's attention, hold the lead in your left hand and the food treat in your right. Place your food hand at the dog's nose and let him lick the treat but not take it from you. Say "Sit" and slowly raise your food hand from in front of the dog's nose up over his head so that he is looking at the ceiling. As he bends his head upward, he will have to bend his knees to maintain his balance. As he bends his knees, he will assume a sit position. At that point, release the food treat and praise lavishly with comments such as "Good dog! Good sit!" Always remember to praise enthusiasti-

The Fila puppy may need a little pressure on his rear quarters to better understand the sit exercise.

Down is the most difficult position to teach a Fila because it is interpreted by the dog as submission.

cally, because dogs relish verbal praise from their owners and feel so proud of themselves whenever they accomplish a behavior.

You will not use food forever in getting the dog to obey your commands. Food is only used to teach new behaviors, and once the dog knows what you want when you give a specific command, you will wean him off the food treats but still maintain the verbal praise. After all, you will always have your voice with you, but there will be many times when you have no food rewards yet expect the dog to obey.

TEACHING DOWN
Teaching the down exercise is easy when you understand how the dog perceives the down position, and it is very difficult when you do not. Dogs perceive the

down position as a submissive posture. Teaching the down exercise using the wrong method can sometimes make the dog develop such a fear of the down that he either runs away when you say "Down" or he attempts to snap at the person who tries to force him down.

Have the dog sit close alongside your left leg, facing in the same direction as you are. Hold the lead in your left hand and a food treat in your right. Now place your left hand lightly on the top of the dog's shoulders where they meet above the spinal cord. Do not push down on the dog's shoulders; simply rest your left hand there so you can guide the dog to lie down close to your left leg rather than to swing away from your side when he drops.

Now place the food hand at the dog's nose, say "Down" very softly (almost a whisper), and slowly lower the food hand to the dog's front feet. When the food

THE LOWDOWN ON DOWN
A dog in jeopardy never lies down. He stays alert on his feet because instinct tells him that he may have to run away or fight for his survival. Therefore, if a dog feels threatened or anxious, he will not lie down. Consequently, it is important to have the dog calm and relaxed as he learns the down exercise.

hand reaches the floor, begin moving it forward along the floor in front of the dog. Keep talking softly to the dog, saying things like, "Do you want this treat? You can do this, good dog." Your reassuring tone of voice will help calm the dog as he tries to follow the food hand in order to get the treat.

When the dog's elbows touch the floor, release the food and praise softly. Try to get the dog to maintain that down position for several seconds before you let him sit up again. The goal here is to get the dog to settle down and not feel threatened in the down position.

TEACHING STAY

It is easy to teach the dog to stay in either a sit or a down position. Again, we use food and praise during the teaching process as we help the dog to understand exactly what it is that we are expecting him to do.

To teach the sit/stay, start with the dog sitting on your left side as before and hold the lead in your left hand. Have a food treat in your right hand and place your food hand at the dog's nose. Say "Stay" and step out on your right foot to stand directly in front of the dog, toe to toe, as he licks and nibbles the treat. Be sure to keep his head facing upward to maintain the sit position. Count to five and then swing around to stand

The stay position, whether seated or standing, is very useful in everyday life. Spend the time to train your dog and he will obey during his entire lifetime.

next to the dog again with him on your left. As soon as you get back to the original position, release the food and praise him.

To teach the down/stay, do the down as previously described. As soon as the dog lies down, say "Stay" and step out on your right

> ### KEEP SMILING
> Never train your dog, puppy or adult, when you are angry or in a sour mood. Dogs are very sensitive to human feelings, especially anger, and if your dog senses that you are angry or upset, he will connect your anger with his training and learn to resent or fear his training sessions.

foot just as you did in the sit/stay. Count to five and then return to stand beside the dog with him on your left side. Release the treat and praise as always.

Within a week or ten days, you can begin to add a bit of distance between you and your dog when you leave him. When you do, use your left hand open with the palm facing the dog as a stay signal, much the same as the hand signal a police officer uses to stop traffic at an intersection. Hold the food treat in your right hand as before, but this time the food is not touching the dog's nose. He will watch the food hand and quickly learn that he is going to get that treat as soon as you return to his side.

When you can stand 1 yard away from your dog for 30 seconds, you can then begin building time and distance in both stays. Eventually, the dog can be expected to remain in the stay position for prolonged periods of time until you return to him or call him to you. Always praise lavishly when he stays.

TEACHING COME

If you make teaching "Come" a fun experience, you should never have a "student" that does not love the game or that fails to come when called. The secret, it seems, is never to teach the word "come."

When your Fila hears your voice, he should learn to pay attention and respond. Teaching the Fila to come to you when called is an essential lesson.

At times when an owner most wants his dog to come when called, the owner is likely upset or anxious and he allows these feelings to come through in the tone of his voice when he calls his dog. Hearing that desperation in his owner's voice, the dog fears the results of going to him and therefore either disobeys outright or runs in the opposite direction. The secret, therefore, is to teach the dog a game and, when you want him to come to you, simply play the game. It is practically a no-fail solution!

To begin, have several members of your family take a few food treats and each go into a different room in the house. Take turns calling the dog, and each person should celebrate the dog's finding him with a treat and lots of happy praise. When a person calls the dog, he is actually inviting the dog to find him and get a treat as a reward for "winning."

A few turns of the "Where are you?" game and the dog will

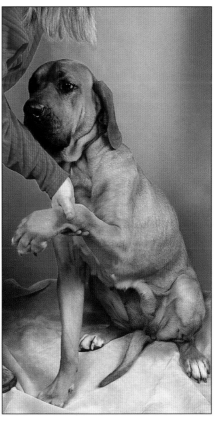

Once you have taught your Fila the basics, such as "sit," it is simple to teach him to "shake hands."

figure out that everyone is playing the game and that each person has a big celebration awaiting his success at locating them. Once he learns to love the game, simply calling out "Where are you?" will bring him running from wherever he is when he hears that all-important question.

The come command is recognized as one of the most important things to teach a dog, so it is interesting to note that there are trainers who work with thousands of dogs and never teach the actual

FETCH!

Play fetching games with your puppy in an enclosed area where he can retrieve his toy and bring it back to you. Always use a toy or object designated just for this purpose. Never use a shoe, sock or other item he may later confuse with those in your closet or underneath your chair.

"COME" ... BACK

Never call your dog to come to you for a correction or scold him when he reaches you. That is the quickest way to turn a come command into "Go away fast!" Dogs think only in the present tense, and your dog will connect the scolding with coming to you, not with the misbehavior of a few moments earlier.

word "come." Yet these dogs will race to respond to a person who uses the dog's name followed by "Where are you?" For example, a woman has a 12-year-old companion dog who went blind, but who never fails to locate her owner when asked, "Where are you?"

Children particularly love to play this game with their dogs. Children can hide in smaller places like a shower stall or bathtub, behind a bed or under a table. The dog needs to work a little bit harder to find these hiding places, but when he does he loves to celebrate with a treat and a tussle with a favorite youngster.

TEACHING HEEL

Heeling means that the dog walks beside the owner without pulling. It takes time and patience on the owner's part to succeed at teaching the dog that he (the owner) will not proceed unless the dog is walking calmly beside him. Pulling out ahead on the lead is definitely not acceptable.

Begin with holding the lead in your left hand as the dog sits beside your left leg. Hold the loop end of the lead in your right hand but keep your left hand short on the lead so it keeps the dog in close next to you.

Say "Heel" and step forward on your left foot. Keep the dog close to you and take three steps. Stop and have the dog sit next to you in what we now call the heel position. Praise verbally, but do not touch the dog. Hesitate a moment and begin again with "Heel," taking three steps and stopping, at which point the dog is told to sit again.

Your goal here is to have the dog walk those three steps without pulling on the lead. When he will walk calmly beside you for three steps without pulling, increase the number of steps you take to five. When he will walk politely beside you while you take five steps, you can increase the length of your walk to ten steps. Keep increasing the length of your stroll until the dog will walk quietly beside you without pulling as long as you want him to heel. When you stop heeling, indicate to the dog that the exercise is over by verbally praising as you pet him and say "OK, good dog." The "OK" is used as a release word, meaning that the exercise is finished and the dog is free to relax.

If you are dealing with a puppy who insists on pulling you around, simply "put on your brakes" and stand your ground until the dog realizes that the two of you are not going anywhere until he is beside you and moving at your pace, not his. It may take some time just standing there to convince the dog that you are the leader and you will be the one to decide on the direction and speed of your travel.

TRAINING TIP

If you begin teaching the heel by taking long walks and letting the dog pull you along, he misinterprets this action as an acceptable form of taking a walk. When you pull back on the lead to counteract his pulling, he reads that tug as a signal to pull even harder!

Each time the dog looks up at you or slows down to give a slack lead between the two of you, quietly praise him and say, "Good heel. Good dog." Eventually, the dog will begin to respond and within a few days he will be walking politely beside you without pulling on the lead. At first, the training sessions should be

A BORN PRODIGY

Occasionally, a dog and owner who have not attended formal classes have been able to earn entry-level titles by obtaining competition rules and regulations from a local kennel club and practicing on their own to a degree of perfection. Obtaining the higher level titles, however, almost always requires extensive training under the tutelage of experienced instructors. In addition, the more difficult levels require more specialized equipment whereas the lower levels do not.

kept short and very positive; soon the dog will be able to walk nicely with you for increasingly longer distances. Remember to give the dog free time and the opportunity to run and play when you are done with heel practice.

WEANING OFF FOOD IN TRAINING

Food is used in training new behaviors, yet once the dog understands what behavior goes with a specific command, it is time to start weaning him off the food treats. At first, give a treat after each exercise. Then, start to give a treat only after

Every time your dog obeys a command, he should be lavishly praised. Your Fila needs encouragement and reinforcement every day of his life, not just during puppyhood.

every other exercise. Mix up the times when you offer a food reward and the times when you only offer praise so that the dog will never know when he is going to receive both food and praise and when he is going to receive only praise. This is called a variable-ratio reward system and it proves successful because there is always the chance that the owner will produce a treat, so the dog never stops trying for that reward. No matter what, *always* give verbal praise.

OBEDIENCE CLASSES

As previously discussed, it is a good idea to enroll in an obedience class if one is available in your area. Many areas have dog clubs that offer basic obedience training as well as preparatory classes for obedience competition. There are also local dog trainers who offer similar classes.

Whether you take formal classes, or choose to teach your dog obedience at home, all Filas need this kind of training. Obedience can be a fun activity for you and your Fila. You can stop at basic obedience or take it much further. Many obedience titles are available, though this would take a lot of dedication on the part of the owner because of the Fila's strong temperament.

At obedience trials, dogs can earn titles at various levels of competition. The beginning levels of competition include basic behaviors such as sit, down, heel, etc. The more advanced levels of competition include jumping, retrieving, scent discrimination and signal work. The advanced levels require a dog and owner to put a lot of time and effort into their training; the titles that can be earned at these levels of competition are very prestigious.

ACTIVITIES FOR YOU AND YOUR FILA

There are many activities you and your Fila Brasileiro can enjoy together. Many Fila owners participate in Fila Brasileiro specialty shows. Breed clubs usually host these shows, which cover more than

OBEDIENCE SCHOOL

A basic obedience beginner's class usually lasts for six to eight weeks. Dog and owner attend an hour-long lesson once a week and practice for a few minutes, several times a day, each day at home. If done properly, the whole procedure will result in a well-mannered dog and an owner who delights in living with a pet that is eager to please and enjoys doing things with his owner.

just conformation. Many specialty shows include other activities such as temperament tests, herding trials and tracking activities.

The temperament test, which is offered at all specialty shows, is a requirement for a Fila to obtain a registered championship title. Any Fila over the age of 12 months can participate in this event, and no training is required. It is a test of the Fila's natural temperament. The dog will be tested on his self-assurance, courage, determination and bravery. One part of the temperament test is a shooting test, in which blanks are fired from a firearm at a distance of five yards from the dog. The dog is judged on his reaction to the

A Fila with a reliable temperament should not react aggressively, though he must be self-confident and brave. This Fila is curious to meet a new and unusual friend.

noise. The other part of the test involves a stranger "attacking" with a stick. The person is not allowed to touch the handler or the dog, but pretends to be attacking them. The dog should attack in front of the handler, without being coached. Some temperament tests also involve testing the Fila's reactions to passing strangers, friendly strangers, strange footing and weird noises.

Other activities that may be offered include herding instinct trials. The trial involves testing a Fila's instinctive herding ability. The Fila Brasileiro enters a pen with livestock to see how it reacts to them. This type of trial is not needed for a championship title; it is only for fun.

If your Fila is a good physical specimen, you can take part in conformation shows as well. In these shows, each dog is judged against the breed standard. This is an activity you can enjoy with your family, though time and money are required to travel to the various shows. Children can also participate, by competing in Junior Showmanship competitions. In these events it is the handler that is being judged, not the dog.

A few very dedicated Fila owners have even worked towards getting their dogs certified for search and rescue work.

Hiking provides excellent exercise for Fila and owner alike. It is essential to keep the Fila on lead at all times.

In this type of work, the dog and owner are trained to help in emergencies. Though the Fila Brasileiro has extraordinary scenting ability, this would still be a challenge for both owner and dog. A Fila would require extensive socialization to be able to perform this type of duty because of the close proximity in which he must work with other dogs and people.

As you can see, there are many things you can enjoy with your Fila Brasileiro. Joining a breed club is a great way to find activities the two of you can do together. A breed club can also put you in touch with other Fila Brasileiro owners, who can share their experiences with you.

Dogs, being mammals like human beings, suffer from many of the same physical illnesses as people. They might even share many of the psychological problems. Since people usually know more about human diseases than canine maladies, many of the terms used in this chapter will be the familiar terms, not necessarily those used by veterinarians. We will still use the term *x-ray*, instead of the more acceptable term *radiograph*. We will also use the familiar term *symptoms*; even though dogs do not have symptoms, which are verbal descriptions of the patient's feelings, dogs have *clinical signs*. Since dogs cannot speak, we have to look for clinical signs...but we still use the term *symptoms* in this book.

As a general rule, medicine is *practiced*. That term is not arbitrary. Medicine is a constantly changing art as we learn more and more about genetics, electronic aids (like CAT scans and MRIs) and new medical developments. There are many dog maladies, like canine hip dysplasia, which are not universally treated in the same manner. Some vets opt for surgery more often than others.

SELECTING A QUALIFIED VET
Your selection of a vet should be based not only upon personality and ability with large-breed dogs but also upon his convenience to your home. You want a vet who is close as you might have emergencies or multiple visits for treatments. You want a vet who has services that you might require, who makes sophisticated pet supplies available and who has a good reputation for ability and responsiveness. There is nothing more frustrating than having to wait a day or more to get a response from a veterinarian.

All vets are licensed and their diplomas and/or certifi-

Before you buy your Fila Brasileiro, meet and interview the vets in your area. Take everything into consideration— discuss his background, specialities, fees, emergency policy, etc.

cates should be displayed in their waiting rooms. There are many veterinary specialties that usually require further studies and internships. There are specialists in heart problems (veterinary cardiologists), skin problems (veterinary dermatologists), teeth and gum problems (veterinary dentists), eye problems (veterinary ophthalmologists), x-rays (veterinary radiologists) and vets who have specialties in bones, muscles or other organs. Most vets do routine surgery such as neutering, stitching up wounds and removing cysts and tumors. When the problem affecting your dog is serious, it is not unusual or impudent to get another medical opinion. You might also want to compare costs among several veterinarians. Sophisticated health care and veterinary services can be very costly. Do not be bashful to discuss these costs with your veterinarian or his staff. It is not infrequent that important decisions are based upon financial considerations.

Breakdown of Veterinary Income by Category

2%	Dentistry
4%	Radiology
12%	Surgery
15%	Vaccinations
19%	Laboratory
23%	Examinations
25%	Medicines

Because the Fila Brasileiro is a rare breed, you may have to educate your veterinarian on the breed. If the vet is not familiar with the breed, you can bring this book and other materials on the breed to be read before your first visit. You can be reassured if the vet has many other big-dog patients.

A typical vet's income, categorized according to services performed. This survey dealt with small-animal (pets) practices.

PREVENTATIVE MEDICINE

It is much easier, less costly and more effective to practice preventative medicine than to fight bouts of illness and disease. Properly bred puppies come from parents that were selected based upon their genetic-disease profile. Their dam should have been vaccinated, free of all internal and external parasites, and properly nourished. The dam can pass on disease resistance to her puppies. This resistance can last

CUSHING'S DISEASE

Cases of hyperactive adrenal glands (Cushing's disease) have been traced to the drinking of highly chlorinated water. Aerate or age your dog's drinking water before offering it.

for eight to ten weeks. She can also pass on parasites and many infections. It is always helpful to learn as much about the dam's health as possible when assessing the condition of her pups.

WEANING TO FIVE MONTHS OLD

Puppies should be weaned by the time they are about two months old. A puppy that remains for at least eight weeks with his dam and littermates usually adapts better to other dogs and people later in his life.

In every case, you should have your newly acquired puppy examined by a veterinarian immediately. Vaccination programs usually begin when the puppy is very young. The puppy will have his teeth examined, and have his skeletal conformation and general health checked prior to certification by the vet. Some puppies of certain breeds have problems with their kneecaps, cataracts and other eye problems, heart murmurs and undescended testicles. They may also have personality problems and your vet might have training in temperament evaluation.

VACCINATION SCHEDULING

Most vaccinations are given by injection and should only be done by a vet. Both he and you should keep a record of the date of the injection, the identification of the vaccine and the

> **NEUTERING/SPAYING**
> Male dogs are castrated. The operation removes both testicles and requires that the dog be anesthetized. Recovery takes about one week. Females are spayed; in this operation, the uterus (womb) and both of the ovaries are removed. This is major surgery, also carried out under general anesthesia, and it usually takes a bitch two weeks to recover.

amount given. Some vets give a first vaccination at eight weeks, but most dog breeders prefer the course not to commence until about ten weeks because of negating any antibodies passed on by the dam. The vaccination scheduling is usually based on a 15-day cycle. You must take your vet's advice as to when to vaccinate as this may differ according to the vaccine used. Most vaccinations immunize your puppy against viruses.

The usual vaccines contain immunizing doses of several different viruses such as distemper, parvovirus, parainfluenza and hepatitis. There are other vaccines available when the puppy is at risk. You should rely upon professional advice. This is especially true for the booster-shot program. Most vaccination programs require a booster when the puppy is a year old, and once a year thereafter. In some

First Aid at a Glance

Burns
Place the affected area under cool water; use ice if only a small area is burnt.

Bee stings/Insect bites
Apply ice to relieve swelling; antihistamine dosed properly.

Animal bites
Clean any bleeding area; apply pressure until bleeding subsides; go to the vet.

Spider bites
Use cold compress and a pressurized pack to inhibit venom's spreading.

Antifreeze poisoning
Induce vomiting with hydrogen peroxide. Seek *immediate* veterinary help!

Fish hooks
Removal best handled by vet; hook must be cut in order to remove.

Snake bites
Pack ice around bite; contact vet quickly; identify snake for proper antivenin.

Car accident
Move dog from roadway with blanket; seek veterinary aid.

Shock
Calm the dog; keep him warm; seek immediate veterinary help.

Nosebleed
Apply cold compress to the nose; apply pressure to any visible abrasion.

Bleeding
Apply pressure above the area; treat wound by applying a cotton pack.

Heat stroke
Submerge dog in cold bath; cool down with fresh air and water; go to the vet.

Frostbite/Hypothermia
Warm the dog with a warm bath, electric blankets or hot water bottles.

Abrasions
Clean the wound and wash out thoroughly with fresh water; apply antiseptic.

 Remember: an injured dog may attempt to bite a helping hand from fear and confusion. Always muzzle the dog before trying to offer assistance.

HEALTH AND VACCINATION SCHEDULE

Age in Weeks:	6th	8th	10th	12th	14th	16th	20-24th	52nd
Worm Control	✔	✔	✔	✔	✔	✔	✔	
Neutering							✔	
Heartworm		✔		✔		✔	✔	
Parvovirus	✔		✔		✔		✔	✔
Distemper		✔		✔		✔		✔
Hepatitis		✔		✔		✔		✔
Leptospirosis								✔
Parainfluenza	✔		✔		✔			✔
Dental Examination		✔					✔	✔
Complete Physical		✔					✔	✔
Coronavirus				✔			✔	✔
Canine Cough	✔							
Hip Dysplasia								✔
Rabies							✔	

Vaccinations are not instantly effective. It takes about two weeks for the dog's immune system to develop antibodies. Most vaccinations require annual booster shots. Your vet should guide you in this regard.

cases, circumstances may require more frequent immunizations.

Canine cough, more formally known as tracheobronchitis, is treated with a vaccine that is sprayed into the dog's nostrils. Canine cough is also usually included in routine vaccination, but this is often not as effective as for other major diseases.

FIVE MONTHS TO ONE YEAR OF AGE
By the time your puppy is five months old, he should have completed his vaccination program. During his physical examination he should be evaluated for the common hip dysplasia plus other diseases of the joints. There are tests to assist in the prediction of these problems.

Unless you intend to breed or show your dog, neutering the puppy at six months of age is recommended. Discuss this with your vet. Neutering has proven to be beneficial to both male and female dogs. Besides the obvious impossibility of pregnancy, it inhibits (but does not prevent) breast cancer in bitches and prostate cancer in male dogs.

Blood tests are performed for heartworm infestation and it is possible that your puppy will be placed on a preventative therapy that will prevent heartworm infection as well as control other internal parasites.

DOGS OLDER THAN ONE YEAR

Continue to visit the veterinarian at least once a year. There is no such disease as old age, but bodily functions do change with age, and the eyes and ears are no longer as efficient. Neither are the internal workings of the liver, kidneys and intestines.

Proper dietary changes, recommended by your veterinarian, can make life more pleasant for the aging Fila Brasileiro and you.

SKIN PROBLEMS IN THE FILA BRASILEIRO

Veterinarians are consulted by dog owners for skin problems more than any other group of diseases or maladies. Dogs' skin is almost as sensitive as human skin and both suffer from almost the same ailments (though the occurrence of acne in dogs is rare). For this reason, veterinary dermatology has developed into a specialty

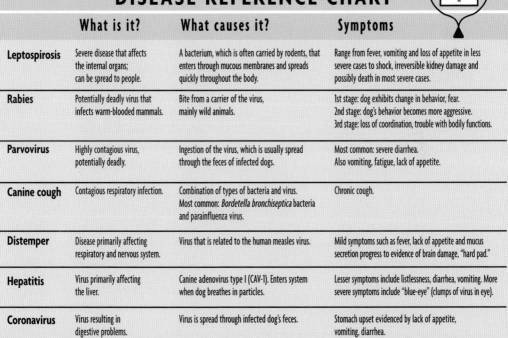

DISEASE REFERENCE CHART

	What is it?	What causes it?	Symptoms
Leptospirosis	Severe disease that affects the internal organs; can be spread to people.	A bacterium, which is often carried by rodents, that enters through mucous membranes and spreads quickly throughout the body.	Range from fever, vomiting and loss of appetite in less severe cases to shock, irreversible kidney damage and possibly death in most severe cases.
Rabies	Potentially deadly virus that infects warm-blooded mammals.	Bite from a carrier of the virus, mainly wild animals.	1st stage: dog exhibits change in behavior, fear. 2nd stage: dog's behavior becomes more aggressive. 3rd stage: loss of coordination, trouble with bodily functions.
Parvovirus	Highly contagious virus, potentially deadly.	Ingestion of the virus, which is usually spread through the feces of infected dogs.	Most common: severe diarrhea. Also vomiting, fatigue, lack of appetite.
Canine cough	Contagious respiratory infection.	Combination of types of bacteria and virus. Most common: *Bordetella bronchiseptica* bacteria and parainfluenza virus.	Chronic cough.
Distemper	Disease primarily affecting respiratory and nervous system.	Virus that is related to the human measles virus.	Mild symptoms such as fever, lack of appetite and mucus secretion progress to evidence of brain damage, "hard pad."
Hepatitis	Virus primarily affecting the liver.	Canine adenovirus type I (CAV-1). Enters system when dog breathes in particles.	Lesser symptoms include listlessness, diarrhea, vomiting. More severe symptoms include "blue-eye" (clumps of virus in eye).
Coronavirus	Virus resulting in digestive problems.	Virus is spread through infected dog's feces.	Stomach upset evidenced by lack of appetite, vomiting, diarrhea.

practiced by many vets.

Since many skin problems have visual symptoms that are almost identical, it requires the skill of an experienced veterinary dermatologist to identify and cure many of the more severe skin disorders. Pet shops sell many treatments for skin problems that are simply directed at symptoms and not the underlying problem(s). Simply put, if your dog is suffering from a skin disorder, seek professional assistance as quickly as possible. As with all diseases, the earlier a problem is identified and treated, the more successful is the cure.

DENTAL HEALTH

A dental examination is in order when the dog is between six months and one year of age so that any permanent teeth that have erupted incorrectly can be corrected. It is important to begin a brushing routine when the dog is a puppy, and be consistent about keeping up with the brushing every week. Durable nylon and safe edible chews should be a part of your puppy's arsenal for good health, good teeth and pleasant breath. The vast majority of dogs three to four years old and older has diseases of the gums from lack of dental attention. Using the various types of dental chews can be very effective in controlling dental plaque.

PARASITE BITES

Many of us are allergic to mosquito bites. The bites itch, erupt and may even become infected. Dogs have the same reaction to fleas, ticks and/or mites. When you feel the prick of the mosquito when it bites you, you have a chance to kill it with your hand. Unfortunately, when your dog is bitten by a flea, tick or mite, he can only scratch it away or bite it. By the time the dog has been bitten, the parasite has done some of its damage. It may also have laid eggs to cause further problems in the future. The itching from parasite bites is probably due to the saliva injected into the site when the parasite sucks the dog's blood.

AUTO-IMMUNE SKIN CONDITIONS

Auto-immune skin conditions are commonly referred to as being allergic to yourself. Allergies, though, usually result in inflammatory reactions to an outside stimulus. Auto-immune diseases cause serious damage to the tissues that are involved.

The best-known auto-immune disease is lupus. It affects people as well as dogs. The symptoms are very variable and may affect the kidneys, bones, blood chemistry and skin. It can be fatal to both dogs and humans, though it is not thought to be transmissible. It is usually successfully treated with cortisone, prednisone or similar corti-costeroids, but extensive use of these drugs can have harmful side effects.

ACRAL LICK GRANULOMA

Many large dogs have a very poorly understood syndrome called acral lick granuloma. The manifestation of the problem is the dog's tireless attack at a specific area of the body, almost always the legs or paws. They lick so intensively that they remove the hair and skin leaving an ugly, large wound. Tiny protuberances, which are outgrowths of new capillaries, bead on the surface of the wound. Owners who notice their dogs' biting and chewing at their extremities should have the veterinarian determine the cause.

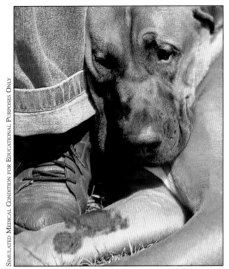

SIMULATED MEDICAL CONDITION FOR EDUCATIONAL PURPOSES ONLY

Sometimes a Fila will lick a spot on his paw until it is raw and bleeds. This is called an acral lick granuloma. Visit your vet if you discover this problem.

If lick granuloma is the cause, although there is no absolute cure, corticosteroids are the most common treatment.

AIRBORNE ALLERGIES

Just as humans have hay fever, rose fever and other fevers from which they suffer during the pollinating season, many dogs suffer from the same allergies. So when the pollen count is high, your dog might suffer. Do not expect them to sneeze and have a runny nose as a human would. Dogs react to pollen allergies the same way they react to fleas—they scratch and bite themselves.

Dogs, like humans, can be tested for allergens. Discuss the testing with a veterinary dermatologist, whom your veterinarian can recommend.

VITAL SIGNS

A dog's normal temperature is 101.5 degrees Fahrenheit. A range of between 100.0 and 102.5 degrees should be considered normal, as each dog's body sets its own temperature. It will be helpful if you take your dog's temperature when you know he is healthy and record it. Then, when you suspect that he is not feeling well, you will have a normal figure to compare the abnormal temperature against.

The normal pulse rate for a dog is between 100 and 125 beats per minute.

12 WAYS TO PREVENT BLOAT

Gastric torsion or bloat is a preventable killer of dogs. We know that bloat affects more large dogs and deep-chested dogs than any other dogs. Bloat can be defined as the rapid accumulation of air in the stomach, causing it to twist or flip over, thereby blocking the entrance and exit. A dog suffering from bloat experiences acute pain and is unable to release the gas. Here are some excellent recommendations to prevent this life-threatening condition.

- Do not provide water at mealtimes, especially for dogs that commonly drink large amounts of water.
- Keep your dog at his proper weight. Avoid overfeeding.
- Limit exercise at least one hour before and two hours after mealtime.
- Avoid stressful or vigorous exercise altogether.
- Provide antacids for any dog with audible stomach motions (borborygmus) or flatulence.
- Feed two or three smaller meals instead of one large meal per day.
- Serve your dog's food and water on a bowl stand so that he does not have to crane his neck to eat.
- Never allow the dog to gulp water.
- Be certain that mealtime is a non-stressful time. Feed the dog alone where he is not competing with a canine or feline housemate for his bowl. Feeding the dog in his crate is an excellent solution.
- For the big gulper, place large toys in the dog's bowl so that he cannot gulp his portions.
- Discuss bloat prevention and preventative surgical methods with your veterinarian.
- If changing your dog's diet, do so gradually.
- Recognize the symptoms of bloat, as time is of the essence. Symptoms include pacing, whining, wretching (with no result), groaning, obvious discomfort.

FOOD PROBLEMS

FOOD ALLERGIES

Dogs are allergic to many foods that are best-sellers and highly recommended by breeders and veterinarians. Changing the brand of food that you buy may not eliminate the problem because the element of the food to which the dog is allergic may also be contained in the new brand.

Recognizing a food allergy is difficult. Humans vomit or have rashes when we eat a food to which we are allergic. Dogs neither vomit nor (usually) develop a rash. Instead they itch, scratch and bite, thus making the diagnosis extremely difficult. While pollen allergies and parasite bites are usually seasonal, food allergies are year-round problems.

FOOD INTOLERANCE

Food intolerance is the inability of the dog to completely digest certain foods. For example, puppies that may have done very well on their mother's milk may not do well on cow's milk. Other ways food intolerance affects the dog are loose bowels, passing gas and stomach pains. These are the only obvious symptoms of food intolerance, thus making diagnosis difficult.

TREATING FOOD PROBLEMS

Handling food allergies and food intolerance yourself is possible. Put your dog on a diet that he has never eaten before. Obviously if he has never eaten this new food, he cannot have been allergic to or intolerant of it. Start with a single ingredient that is not in the dog's diet at the present time. Ingredients like chopped beef or chicken are common in dog's diets, so try something more exotic like rabbit, pheasant or another source of protein. Keep the dog on this diet (with no additives) for a month. If the symptoms of food allergy or intolerance disappear, chances are that you have defined the cause.

Do not think that the single ingredient cured the problem. You still must find a suitable diet and ascertain which ingredient in the old diet was objectionable. This is most easily done by adding ingredients to the new diet one at a time until the problem is solved. Let the dog stay on the modified diet for a month before you add another ingredient.

An alternative method is to study the ingredients in the diet to which your dog is allergic or intolerant. Identify the main ingredient in this diet and eliminate the main ingredient by buying a different food that does not have that ingredient. Keep experimenting until the symptoms disappear after one month on the new diet.

A SKUNKY PROBLEM

Have you noticed your dog dragging his rump along the floor? If so, it is likely that his anal sacs are impacted or possibly infected. The anal sacs are small pouches located on both sides of the anus under the skin and muscles. They are about the size and shape of a grape and contain a foul-smelling liquid. Their contents are usually emptied when the dog has a bowel movement but, if not emptied completely, they will impact, which will cause your dog much pain. Fortunately, your veterinarian can tend to this problem easily by draining the sacs for the dog. Be aware that your dog might also empty his anal sacs in cases of extreme fright.

A male dog flea, *Ctenocephalides canis.*

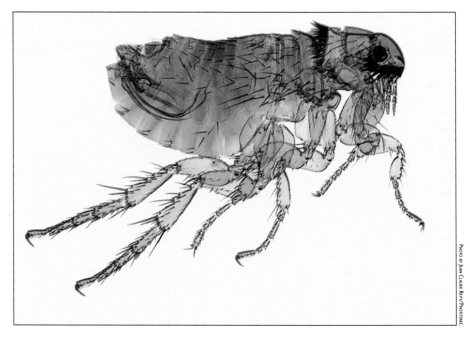

PHOTO BY JEAN CLAUDE REVY/PHOTOTAKE

EXTERNAL PARASITES

FLEAS

Of all the problems to which dogs are prone, none is more well known and frustrating than fleas. Flea infestation is relatively simple to cure but difficult to prevent. Parasites that are harbored inside the body are a bit more difficult to eradicate but they are easier to control.

To control flea infestation, you have to understand the flea's life cycle. Fleas are often thought of as a summertime problem, but centrally heated homes have changed the patterns and fleas can be found at any time of the year. The most effective method of flea control is a two-stage approach: one stage to kill the adult fleas, and the other to control the development of pre-adult fleas. Unfortunately, no single active ingredient is effective against all stages of the life cycle.

**FLEA KILLER CAUTION—
"POISON"**

Flea-killers are poisonous. You should not spray these toxic chemicals on areas of a dog's body that he licks, including his genitals and his face. Flea killers taken internally are a better answer, but check with your vet in case internal therapy is not advised for your dog.

LIFE CYCLE STAGES

During its life, a flea will pass through four life stages: egg, larva, pupa or nymph and adult. The adult stage is the most visible and irritating stage of the flea life cycle, and this is why the majority of flea-control products concentrate on this stage. The fact is that adult fleas account for only 1% of the total flea population, and the other 99% exist in pre-adult stages, i.e., eggs, larvae and nymphs. The pre-adult stages are barely visible to the naked eye.

THE LIFE CYCLE OF THE FLEA

Eggs are laid on the dog, usually in quantities of about 20 or 30, several times a day. The adult female flea must have a blood meal before each egg-laying session. When first laid, the eggs will cling to the dog's hair, as the eggs are still moist. However, they will quickly dry out and fall from the dog, especially if the dog moves around or scratches. Many eggs will fall off in the dog's favorite area or an area in which he spends a lot of time, such as his bed.

Once the eggs fall from the dog onto the carpet or furniture, they will hatch into larvae. This takes from one to ten days. Larvae are not particularly mobile and will usually travel only a few inches from where they hatch. However, they do have a tendency to move away from bright light and heavy

EN GARDE:
CATCHING FLEAS OFF GUARD!
Consider the following ways to arm yourself against fleas:
- Add a small amount of pennyroyal or eucalyptus oil to your dog's bath. These natural remedies repel fleas.
- Supplement your dog's food with fresh garlic (minced or grated) and a hearty amount of brewer's yeast, both of which ward off fleas.
- Use a flea comb on your dog daily. Submerge fleas in a cup of bleach to kill them quickly.
- Confine the dog to only a few rooms to limit the spread of fleas in the home.
- Vacuum daily...and get all of the crevices! Dispose of the bag every few days until the problem is under control.
- Wash your dog's bedding daily. Cover cushions where your dog sleeps with towels, and wash the towels often.

traffic—under furniture and behind doors are common places to find high quantities of flea larvae.

The flea larvae feed on dead organic matter, including adult flea feces, until they are ready to change into adult fleas. Fleas will usually remain as larvae for around seven days. After this period, the larvae will pupate into protective pupae. While inside the pupae, the larvae will undergo metamorphosis and change into

Fleas have been measured as being able to jump 300,000 times and can jump over 150 times their length in any direction, including straight up.

adult fleas. This can take as little time as a few days, but the adult fleas can remain inside the pupae waiting to hatch for up to two years. The pupae are signaled to hatch by certain stimuli, such as physical pressure—the pupae's being stepped on, heat from an animal's lying on the pupae or increased carbon-dioxide levels and vibrations—indicating that a suitable host is available.

Once hatched, the adult flea must feed within a few days. Once the adult flea finds a host, it will not leave voluntarily. It only becomes dislodged by grooming or the host animal's scratching. The adult flea will remain on the

host for the duration of its life unless forcibly removed.

TREATING THE ENVIRONMENT AND THE DOG

Treating fleas should be a two-pronged attack. First, the environment needs to be treated; this includes carpets and furniture, especially the dog's bedding and areas underneath furniture. The environment should be treated with a household spray containing an Insect Growth Regulator (IGR) and an insecticide to kill the adult fleas. Most IGRs are effective against eggs and larvae; they actually mimic the fleas' own hormones and stop the eggs and larvae from developing into adult fleas. There are currently no treatments available to attack the pupa stage of the life cycle, so the adult insecticide is used to kill the newly hatched adult fleas before they find a host. Most IGRs are active for many months, while adult insecticides are only active

A scanning electron micrograph of a dog or cat flea, *Ctenocephalides*, magnified more than 100x. This image has been colorized for effect.

THE LIFE CYCLE OF THE FLEA

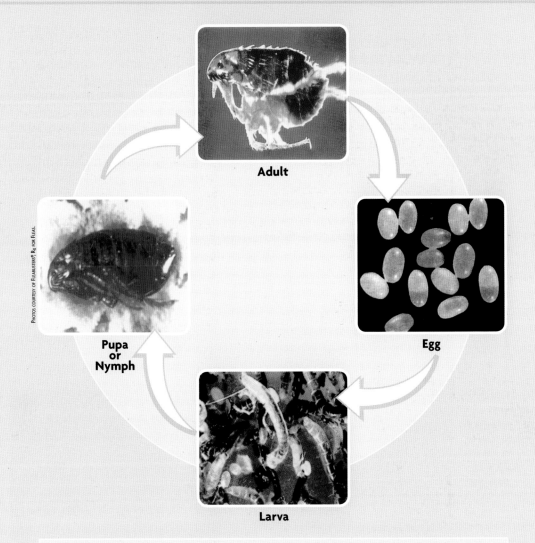

Adult

Egg

Larva

Pupa or Nymph

PHOTOS COURTESY OF FLEABUSTERS® RX FOR FLEAS.

Fleas have been around for millions of years and have adapted to changing host animals. They are able to go through a complete life cycle in less than one month or they can extend their lives to almost two years by remaining as pupae or cocoons. They do not need blood or any other food for up to 20 months.

> ## INSECT GROWTH REGULATOR (IGR)
>
> Two types of products should be used when treating fleas—a product to treat the pet and a product to treat the home. Adult fleas represent less than 1% of the flea population. The pre-adult fleas (eggs, larvae and pupae) represent more than 99% of the flea population and are found in the environment; it is in the case of pre-adult fleas that products containing an Insect Growth Regulator (IGR) should be used in the home.
>
> IGRs are a new class of compounds used to prevent the development of insects. They do not kill the insect outright, but instead use the insect's biology against it to stop it from completing its growth. Products that contain methoprene are the world's first and leading IGRs. Used to control fleas and other insects, this type of IGR will stop flea larvae from developing and protect the house for up to seven months.

The American dog tick, *Dermacentor variabilis*, is probably the most common tick found on dogs. Look at the strength in its eight legs! No wonder it's hard to detach them.

is to apply an adult insecticide to the dog. Traditionally, this would be in the form of a collar or a spray, but more recent innovations include digestible insecticides that poison the fleas when they ingest the dog's blood. Alternatively, there are drops that, when placed on the back of the dog's neck, spread throughout the hair and skin to kill adult fleas.

TICKS

Though not as common as fleas, ticks are found all over the tropical and temperate world. They don't bite, like fleas; they harpoon. They dig their sharp proboscis (nose) into the dog's skin and drink the blood. Their only food and drink is dog's

for a few days.

When treating with a house-hold spray, it is a good idea to vacuum before applying the product. This stimulates as many pupae as possible to hatch into adult fleas. The vacuum cleaner should also be treated with an insecticide to prevent the eggs and larvae that have been collected in the vacuum bag from hatching.

The second stage of treatment

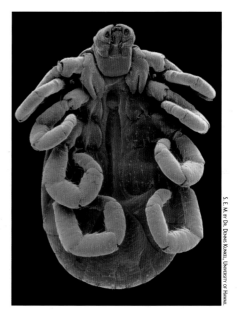

S. E. M. BY DR. DENNIS KUNKEL, UNIVERSITY OF HAWAII

blood. Dogs can get Lyme disease, Rocky Mountain spotted fever, tick bite paralysis and many other diseases from ticks. They may live where fleas are found and they like to hide in cracks or seams in walls. They are controlled the same way fleas are controlled.

The American dog tick, *Dermacentor variabilis*, may well be the most common dog tick in many geographical areas, especially those areas where the climate is hot and humid. Most dog ticks have life expectancies of a week to six months, depending upon climatic conditions. They can neither jump nor fly, but they can crawl slowly and can range up to 16 feet to reach a sleeping or unsuspecting dog.

MITES

Just as fleas and ticks can be problematic for your dog, mites can also lead to an itchy nuisance. Microscopic in size, mites are related to ticks and generally take up permanent residence on their host animal—in this case, your dog! The term *mange* refers to any infestation caused by one of the mighty mites, of which there are six varieties that concern dog owners.

Demodex mites cause a condition known as demodicosis (sometimes called red mange or

DEER-TICK CROSSING

The great outdoors may be fun for your dog, but it also is a home to dangerous ticks. Deer ticks carry a bacterium known as *Borrelia burgdorferi* and are most active in the autumn and spring. When infections are caught early, penicillin and tetracycline are effective antibiotics, but, if left untreated, the bacteria may cause neurological, kidney and cardiac problems as well as long-term trouble with walking and painful joints.

S. E. M. BY DR. ANDREW SPIELMAN/PHOTOTAKE.

PHOTO BY DR. DENNIS KUNKEL, UNIVERSITY OF HAWAII.

The head of an American dog tick, *Dermacentor variabilis*, enlarged and colorized for effect.

The mange mite, *Psoroptes bovis*, can infest cattle and other domestic animals.

PHOTO BY JAMES HANKEN/YOAV/PHOTOTAKE.

follicular mange), in which the mites live in the dog's hair follicles and sebaceous glands in larger-than-normal numbers. This type of mange is commonly passed from the dam to her puppies and usually shows up on the puppies' muzzles, though demodicosis is not transferable from one normal dog to another. Most dogs recover from this type of mange without any treatment, though topical therapies are commonly prescribed by the vet.

Human lice look like dog lice; the two are closely related.

PHOTO BY DWIGHT R. KUHN.

The *Cheyletiellosis* mite is the hook-mouthed culprit associated with "walking dandruff," a condition that affects dogs as well as cats and rabbits. This mite lives on the surface of the animal's skin and is readily transferable through direct or indirect contact with an affected animal. The dandruff is present in the form of scaly skin, which may or may not be itchy. If not treated, this mange can affect a whole kennel of dogs and can be spread to humans as well.

The *Sarcoptes* mite causes intense itching on the dog in the form of a condition known as scabies or sarcoptic mange. The cycle of the *Sarcoptes* mite lasts about three weeks, and the mites live in the top layer of the dog's skin (epidermis), preferably in areas with little hair. Scabies is highly contagious and can be passed to humans. Sometimes an allergic reaction to the mite worsens the severe itching associated with sarcoptic mange.

Ear mites, *Otodectes cynotis,* lead to otodectic mange, which most commonly affects the outer ear canal of the dog, though other areas can be affected as well. Dogs with ear-mite infestation commonly scratch at their ears, causing further irritation, and shake their heads. Dark brown droppings in the outer ear confirm the diagnosis. Your vet can prescribe a treatment to flush out the ears and kill any eggs in the ears. A complete month of treatment is necessary to cure the mange.

Two other mites, less common in dogs, include *Dermanyssus gallinae* (the poultry or red mite) and *Eutrombicula alfreddugesi* (the North American mite associated with trombiculidiasis or chigger infestation). The poultry mite frequently lives on chickens, but can transfer to dogs who spend time near farm animals. Chigger infestation affects dogs in the

DO NOT MIX

Never mix parasite-control products without first consulting your vet. Some products can become toxic when combined with others and can cause fatal consequences.

NOT A DROP TO DRINK

Never allow your dog to swim in polluted water or public areas where water quality can be suspect. Even perfectly clear water can harbor parasites, many of which can cause serious to fatal illnesses in canines. Areas inhabited by waterfowl and other wildlife are especially dangerous.

Central US who have exposure to woodlands. The types of mange caused by both of these mites are treatable by vets.

INTERNAL PARASITES

Most animals—fishes, birds and mammals, including dogs and humans—have worms and other parasites that live inside their bodies. According to Dr. Herbert R. Axelrod, the fish pathologist, there are two kinds of parasites: dumb and smart. The smart parasites live in peaceful cooperation with their hosts (symbiosis), while the dumb parasites kill their hosts. Most worm infections are relatively easy to control. If they are not controlled, they weaken the host dog to the point that other medical problems occur, but they do not kill the host as dumb parasites would.

A brown dog tick, *Rhipicephalus sanguineus*, is an uncommon but annoying tick found on dogs.
PHOTO BY CAROLINA BIOLOGICAL SUPPLY/PHOTOTAKE.

PHOTO BY CAROLINA BIOLOGICAL SUPPLY/PHOTOTAKE.

The roundworm *Rhabditis* can infect both dogs and humans.

ROUNDWORMS

Average-size dogs can pass 1,360,000 roundworm eggs every day. For example, if there were only 1 million dogs in the world, the world would be saturated with thousands of tons of dog feces. These feces would contain around 15,000,000,000 roundworm eggs.

Up to 31% of home yards and children's sand boxes in the US contain roundworm eggs.

Flushing dog's feces down the toilet is not a safe practice because the usual sewage treatments do not destroy roundworm eggs.

Infected puppies start shedding roundworm eggs at three weeks of age. They can be infected by their mother's milk.

The roundworm, *Ascaris lumbricoides.*

PHOTO BY DWIGHT R. KUHN.

ROUNDWORMS

The roundworms that infect dogs are known scientifically as *Toxocara canis*. They live in the dog's intestines and shed eggs continually. It has been estimated that a dog produces about 6 or more ounces of feces every day. Each ounce of feces averages hundreds of thousands of roundworm eggs. There are no known areas in which dogs roam that do not contain roundworm eggs. The greatest danger of roundworms is that they infect people, too! It is wise to have your dog tested regularly for roundworms.

In young puppies, roundworms cause bloated bellies, diarrhea, coughing and vomiting, and are transmitted from the dam (through blood or milk). Affected puppies will not appear as animated as normal puppies. The worms appear spaghetti-like, measuring as long as 6 inches. Adult dogs can acquire roundworms through coprophagia (eating contaminated feces) or by killing rodents that carry roundworms.

Roundworm infection can kill puppies and cause severe problems in adults, as the hatched larvae travel to the lungs and trachea through the bloodstream. Cleanliness is the best preventative for roundworms. Always pick up after your dog and dispose of feces in appropriate receptacles.

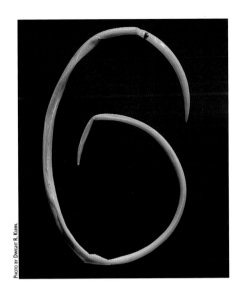

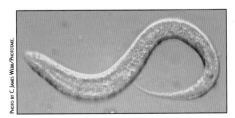

HOOKWORMS

In the United States, dog owners have to be concerned about four different species of hookworm, the most common and most serious of which is *Ancylostoma caninum,* which prefers warm climates. The others are *Ancylostoma braziliense, Ancylostoma tubaeforme* and *Uncinaria stenocephala,* the latter of which is a concern to dogs living in the Northern US and Canada, as this species prefers cold climates. Hookworms are dangerous to humans as well as to dogs and cats, and can be the cause of severe anemia due to iron deficiency. The worm uses its teeth to attach itself to the dog's intestines and changes the site of its attachment about six times per day. Each time the worm

repositions itself, the dog loses blood and can become anemic. *Ancylostoma caninum* is the most likely of the four species to cause anemia in the dog.

Symptoms of hookworm infection include dark stools, weight loss, general weakness, pale coloration and anemia, as well as possible skin problems. Fortunately, hookworms are easily purged from the affected dog with a number of medications that have proven effective. Discuss these with your vet. Most heartworm preventatives include a hookworm insecticide as well.

Owners also must be aware that hookworms can infect humans, who can acquire the larvae through exposure to contaminated feces. Since the worms cannot complete their life cycle on a human, the worms simply infest the skin and cause irritation. This condition is known as cutaneous larva migrans syndrome. As a preventative, use disposable gloves or a "poop-scoop" to pick up your dog's droppings and prevent your dog (or neighborhood cats) from defecating in children's play areas.

The hookworm, *Ancylostoma caninum*.

The infective stage of the hookworm larva.

TAPEWORMS

Humans, rats, squirrels, foxes, coyotes, wolves and domestic dogs are all susceptible to tapeworm infection. Except in humans, tapeworms are usually not a fatal infection. Infected individuals can harbor 1000 parasitic worms.

Tapeworms, like some other types of worm, are hermaphroditic, meaning male and female in the same worm.

If dogs eat infected rats or mice, or anything else infected with tapeworm, they get the tapeworm disease. One month after attaching to a dog's intestine, the worm starts shedding eggs. These eggs are infective immediately. Infective eggs can live for a few months without a host animal.

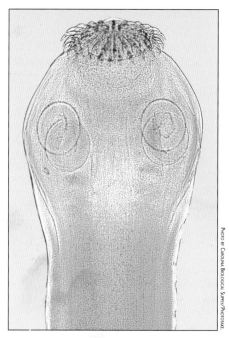

The head and rostellum (the round prominence on the scolex) of a tapeworm, which infects dogs and humans.

PHOTO BY CAROLINA BIOLOGICAL SUPPLY/PHOTOTAKE.

TAPEWORMS

There are many species of tapeworm, all of which are carried by fleas! The most common tapeworm affecting dogs is known as *Dipylidium caninum*. The dog eats the flea and starts the tapeworm cycle. Humans can also be infected with tapeworms—so don't eat fleas! Fleas are so small that your dog could pass them onto your hands, your plate or your food and thus make it possible for you to ingest a flea that is carrying tapeworm eggs.

While tapeworm infection is not life-threatening in dogs (smart parasite!), it can be the cause of a very serious liver disease for humans. About 50% of the humans infected with *Echinococcus multilocularis*, a type of tapeworm that causes alveolar hydatid, perish.

WHIPWORMS

In North America, whipworms are counted among the most common parasitic worms in dogs. The whipworm's scientific name is *Trichuris vulpis*. These worms attach themselves in the lower parts of the intestine, where they feed. Affected dogs may only experience upset tummies, colic and diarrhea. These worms, however, can live for months or years in the dog, beginning their larval stage in the small intestine, spending their adult stage in the large intestine and finally passing infective eggs through the dog's feces. The only way to detect whipworms is through a fecal examination, though this is not always foolproof. Treatment for whipworms is tricky, due to the worms' unusual life-cycle pattern, and very often dogs are reinfected due to exposure to infective eggs on the ground. The whipworm eggs can survive in the environment for as long as five years; thus, cleaning up droppings in your own backyard as well as in public places is essential for sanitation purposes and the health of your dog and others.

THREADWORMS

Though less common than round-worms, hookworms and those previously mentioned, thread-worms concern dog owners in the Southwestern US and Gulf Coast area where the climate is hot and humid. Living in the small intes-tine of the dog, this worm measures a mere 2 millimeters and is round in shape. Like that of the whipworm, the threadworm's life cycle is very complex and the eggs and larvae are passed through the feces. A deadly disease in humans, *Strongyloides* readily infects people, and the handling of feces is the most common means of trans-mission. Threadworms are most often seen in young puppies; bloody diarrhea and pneumonia are symptoms. Sick puppies must be isolated and treated immedi-ately; vets recommend a follow-up treatment one month later.

HEARTWORM PREVENTATIVES

There are many heartworm preventatives on the market, many of which are sold at your veterinarian's office. These products can be given daily or monthly, depending on the manufacturer's instructions. All of these preventatives contain chemical insecticides directed at killing heartworms, which leads to some controversy among dog owners. In effect, heartworm preventatives are neces-sary evils, though you should determine how necessary based on your pet's lifestyle. There is no doubt that heartworm is a dreadful disease that threatens the lives of dogs. However, the likelihood of your dog's being bitten by an infected mosquito is slim in most places, and a mosquito-repellent (or an herbal remedy such as Wormwood or Black Walnut) is much safer for your dog and will not compromise his immune system (the way heartworm preventatives will). Should you decide to use the tradi-tional preventative "medications," you can consider giving the pill every other or third month. Since the toxins in the pill will kill the heartworms at all stages of develop-ment, the pill would be effective in killing larvae, nymphs or adults, and it takes four months for the larvae to reach the adult stage. Thus, there is no rationale to poison-ing the dog's system on a monthly basis. Lastly, do not give the pill during the winter months, since there are no mosquitoes around to pass on their infection, unless you live in a tropical environment.

Life Cycle of the Heartworm

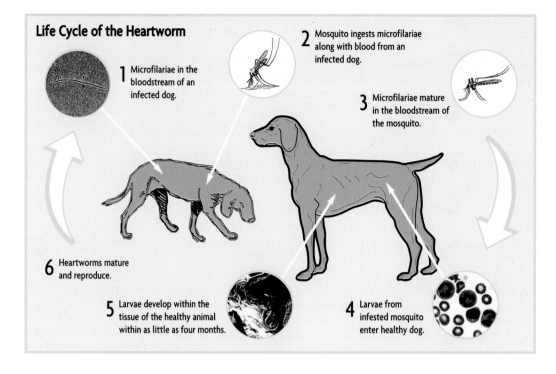

1 Microfilariae in the bloodstream of an infected dog.

2 Mosquito ingests microfilariae along with blood from an infected dog.

3 Microfilariae mature in the bloodstream of the mosquito.

4 Larvae from infested mosquito enter healthy dog.

5 Larvae develop within the tissue of the healthy animal within as little as four months.

6 Heartworms mature and reproduce.

HEARTWORMS

Heartworms are thin, extended worms up to 12 inches long, which live in a dog's heart and the major blood vessels surrounding it. Dogs may have up to 200 worms. Symptoms may be loss of energy, loss of appetite, coughing, the development of a pot belly and anemia.

Heartworms are transmitted by mosquitoes. The mosquito drinks the blood of an infected dog and takes in larvae with the blood. The larvae, called microfilariae, develop within the body of the mosquito and are passed on to the next dog bitten after the larvae mature. It takes two to three weeks for the larvae to develop to the infective stage within the body of the mosquito. Dogs are usually treated at about six weeks of age and maintained on a prophylactic dose given monthly.

Blood testing for heartworms is not necessarily indicative of how seriously your dog is infected. Although this is a dangerous disease, it is not easy for a dog to be infected. Discuss the various preventatives with your vet, as there are many different types now available. Together you can decide on a safe course of prevention for your dog.

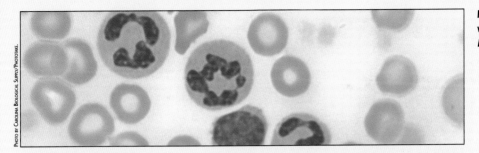

Magnified heart-worm larvae, *Dirofilaria immitis.*

Photo by Carolina Biological Supply/Phototake.

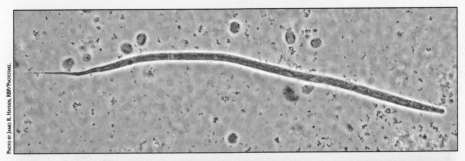

Heartworm, *Dirofilaria immitis.*

Photo by James R. Hayden, RBP/Phototake.

The heart of a dog infected with canine heart-worm, *Dirofilaria immitis.*

Photo by James R. Hayden, RBP/Phototake.

HOMEOPATHY:
an alternative
to conventional
medicine

"Less is Most"

Using this principle, the strength of a homeopathic remedy is measured by the number of serial dilutions that were undertaken to create it. The greater the number of serial dilutions, the greater the strength of the homeopathic remedy. The potency of a remedy that has been made by making a dilution of 1 part in 100 parts (or 1/100) is 1c or 1cH. If this remedy is subjected to a series of further dilutions, each one being 1/100, a more dilute and stronger remedy is produced. If the remedy is diluted in this way six times, it is called 6c or 6cH. A dilution of 6c is 1 part in 1,000,000,000,000. In general, higher potencies in more frequent doses are better for acute symptoms and lower potencies in more infrequent doses are more useful for chronic, long-standing problems.

CURING OUR DOGS NATURALLY

Holistic medicine means treating the whole animal as a unique, perfect, living being. Generally, holistic treatments do not suppress the symptoms that the body naturally produces, as do most medications prescribed by conventional doctors and vets. Holistic methods seek to cure disease by regaining balance and harmony in the patient's environment. Some of these methods include use of nutritional therapy, herbs, flower essences, aromatherapy, acupuncture, massage, chiropractic and, of course, the most popular holistic approach, homeopathy.

Homeopathy is a theory or system of treating illness with small doses of substances which, if administered in larger quantities, would produce the symptoms that the patient already has. This approach is often described as "like cures like." Although modern veterinary medicine is geared toward the "quick fix," homeopathy relies on the belief that, given the time, the body is able to heal itself and return to its natural, healthy state.

Choosing a remedy to cure a problem in our dogs is the difficult part of homeopathy. Consult with your vet for a professional diagnosis of your dog's symptoms. Often these symptoms require immediate conventional care. If your vet is willing and knowledgeable, you may attempt a homeopathic remedy. Be aware that cortisone prevents homeopathic remedies from working. There are hundreds of possibilities and combinations to cure many problems in dogs, from basic physical problems such as excessive shedding, fleas or other parasites, unattractive doggy odor, bad breath, upset tummy, obesity, dry, oily or dull coat, diarrhea, ear problems or eye discharge (including tears and dry or mucousy matter), to behavioral abnormalities such as fear of loud noises, habitual licking, poor appetite, excessive barking and various phobias. From alumina to zincum metallicum, the remedies span the planet and the imagination…from flowers and weeds to chemicals, insect droppings, diesel smoke and volcanic ash.

Using "Like to Treat Like"

Unlike conventional medicines that suppress symptoms, homeopathic remedies treat illnesses with small doses of substances that, if administered in larger quantities, would produce the symptoms that the patient already has. While the same homeopathic remedy can be used to treat different symptoms in different dogs, here are some interesting remedies and their uses.

Apis Mellifica
(made from honey bee venom) can be used for allergies or to reduce swelling that occurs in acutely infected kidneys.

Diesel Smoke
can be used to help control travel sickness.

Calcarea Fluorica
(made from calcium fluoride, which helps harden bone structure) can be useful in treating hard lumps in tissues.

Natrum Muriaticum
(made from common salt, sodium chloride) is useful in treating thin, thirsty dogs.

Nitricum Acidum
(made from nitric acid) is used for symptoms you would expect to see from contact with acids, such as lesions, especially where the skin joins the linings of body orifices or openings such as the lips and nostrils.

Symphytum
(made from the herb Knitbone, *Symphytum officianale*) is used to encourage bones to heal.

Urtica Urens
(made from the common stinging nettle) is used in treating painful, irritating rashes.

Number-One Killer Disease in Dogs: CANCER

In every age, there is a word associated with a disease or plague that causes humans to shudder. In the 21st century, that word is "cancer." Just as cancer is the leading cause of death in humans, it claims nearly half the lives of dogs that die from a natural disease as well as half the dogs that die over the age of ten years.

Described as a genetic disease, cancer becomes a greater risk as the dog ages. Vets and dog owners have become increasingly aware of the threat of cancer to dogs. Statistics reveal that one dog in every five will develop cancer, the most common of which is skin cancer. Many cancers, including prostate, ovarian and breast cancer, can be avoided by spaying and neutering our dogs around the age of six months.

Early detection of cancer can save or extend a dog's life, so it is absolutely vital for owners to have their dogs examined by a qualified vet or oncologist immediately upon detection of any abnormality. Certain dietary guidelines have also proven to reduce the onset and spread of cancer. Foods based on fish rather than beef, due to the presence of Omega-3 fatty acids, are recommended. Other amino acids such as glutamine have significant benefits for canines, particularly those breeds that show a greater susceptibility to cancer.

Cancer management and treatments promise hope for future generations of canines. Since the disease is genetic, breeders should never breed a dog whose parents, grandparents and any related siblings have developed cancer. It is difficult to know whether to exclude an otherwise healthy dog from a breeding program as the disease does not manifest itself until the dog's senior years.

RECOGNIZE CANCER WARNING SIGNS

Since early detection can possibly rescue your dog from becoming a cancer statistic, it is essential for owners to recognize the possible signs and seek the assistance of a qualified professional.

- Abnormal bumps or lumps that continue to grow
- Bleeding or discharge from any body cavity
- Persistent stiffness or lameness
- Recurrent sores or sores that do not heal
- Inappetence
- Breathing difficulties
- Weight loss
- Bad breath or odors
- General malaise and fatigue
- Eating and swallowing problems
- Difficulty urinating and defecating

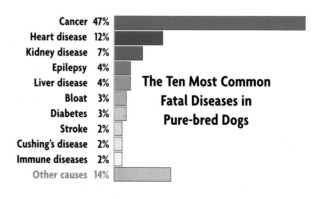

Cancer	47%
Heart disease	12%
Kidney disease	7%
Epilepsy	4%
Liver disease	4%
Bloat	3%
Diabetes	3%
Stroke	2%
Cushing's disease	2%
Immune diseases	2%
Other causes	14%

The Ten Most Common Fatal Diseases in Pure-bred Dogs

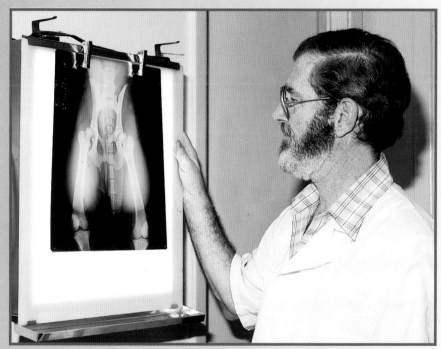

(Above) A veterinarian evaluating a dog's x-ray for hip dysplasia. Diagnosis can only be made using x-ray techniques, which are interpreted (read) by a suitably trained veterinarian.
(Below) The lateral (far left illustration) and flexed lateral (far right illustration) of a three-year-old dog's elbow manifesting elbow dysplasia with associated problems (acute, severe weight-bearing lameness of the right forelimb).

PHOTO COURTESY OF M.A. STEVENSON, DVM / THE JOURNAL OF THE AMERICAN VETERINAY ASSOCIATION.

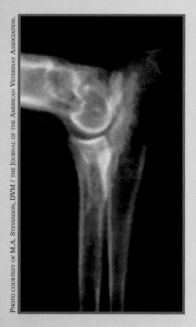
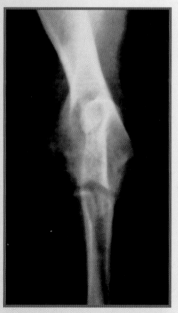
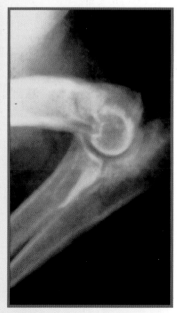

FILA BRASILEIRO

When you purchased your Fila Brasileiro, you should have made it clear to the breeder whether you wanted one just as a faithful companion and pet, or if you hoped to be buying a Fila with show prospects. No reputable breeder will sell you a young puppy saying that he is definitely of show quality for so much can go wrong during the early weeks and months of a puppy's development. If you plan to show, what you will hopefully have acquired is a puppy with "show potential."

To the novice, exhibiting a Fila Brasileiro in the show ring may look easy but it usually takes a lot of hard work and devotion to do top winning at a show such as the prestigious World Dog Show, not to mention a little luck too!

The first concept that the canine novice learns when watching a dog show is that each dog first competes against members of his own breed. Once the judge has selected the best member of each breed, provided that the show is judged on the Group system, then that chosen dog will compete with other dogs in his group.

Finally, the best of each group will compete for Best in Show.

The second concept that you must understand is that the dogs are not actually competing against one another. The judge compares each dog against the breed standard, which is a written description of the ideal specimen of the breed. While some early breed standards were indeed based on specific dogs that were famous or popular, many dedicated enthusiasts say that a perfect specimen, described in the standard, has never been bred. Thus the "perfect" dog has never walked into a show ring, has never been bred and, to the woe of dog breeders around the globe, does not exist. Breeders attempt to get as close to this ideal as possible, with every litter, but theoretically the "perfect" dog is so elusive that it is impossible. (And if the "perfect" dog were born, breeders and judges would never agree that it was indeed "perfect.")

Showing a Fila is not as easy as showing one of the more common breeds. Because the Fila Brasileiro is still considered a rare breed, you will probably have to travel to most shows. This requires more time and money on your part. If you are interested in exploring dog shows in general, your best bet is to join a breed club. These clubs often host specialties (shows for Filas only), puppy matches, judges' seminars and various trials, all of which could be of interest, even if you are only an onlooker. Clubs also send out newsletters and some organize training days in order that people may learn more about their chosen breed. To locate the nearest breed club for you, contact the Fédération Cynologique Internationale or the American Rare Breed Association.

Established in 1911, the Fédération Cynologique Internationale (FCI) represents the "world kennel club." This international body brings uniformity to the breeding, judging and showing of purebred dogs. Although the FCI originally included only five European nations: France, Germany, Holland, Austria and Belgium (which remains its headquarters), the organization today embraces nations on six continents and recognizes well over 300 breeds of pure-bred dog. There are three titles attainable through the FCI: the International Champion, which is the most prestigious; the International Beauty Champion, which is based on aptitude certificates in different countries; and the International Trial Champion, which is based on achievement in obedience trials in different countries. Dog fanciers from around the world participate in these impressive canine spectacles, the largest of which is the World Dog Show, hosted in a different country each year. The FCI sponsors both national and international shows. The hosting country determines the judging system and breed standards are always based on the breed's country of origin.

The FCI is divided into ten groups. The Fila Brasileiro belongs to Group II. At the World Dog Show, the following classes are offered for each breed: Puppy Class (6–9 months), Junior Class (9–18 months), Open Class (15 months or older) and Champion Class. A dog can be awarded a classification of Excellent, Very

Gaiting the Fila in the show ring, to demonstrate the dog's effortless movement and drive, requires practice and skill.

Good, Good, Sufficient and Not Sufficient. Puppies can be awarded classifications of Very Promising, Promising or Not Promising. Four placements are made in each class. After all classes are judged, a Best of Breed is selected. Other special groups and classes may also be shown. Each exhibitor showing a dog receives a written evaluation from the judge. Besides the World Dog Show, you can exhibit your Fila at specialty shows held by different Fila Brasileiro or rare-breed clubs. Specialty shows may have their own regulations.

Before you actually step into the ring, you would be well advised to sit back and observe the judge's ring procedure. If it is your first time in the ring, do not be over-anxious and run to the front of the line. It is much better to stand back and study how the exhibitor in front of you is performing. The judge asks each handler to "stack" the dog, hopefully showing the dog off to his best advantage. The judge will observe the dog from a distance and from different angles, approach the dog, check his teeth, overall structure, alertness and muscle tone, as well as consider how well the dog

"conforms" to the standard. The judge also will have the exhibitor move the dog around the ring in some pattern that he should specify. The Fila's temperament is also evaluated by the judge. Finally the judge will give the dog one last look before moving on to the next exhibitor.

If you are not in the top three at your first show, do not be discouraged. Be patient and consistent and you may eventually find yourself in the winning lineup. Remember that the winners were once in your shoes and have devoted many hours and much money to earn the placement. If you find that your dog is losing every time and never getting a nod, it may be time to consider a different dog sport or just enjoy your Fila Brasileiro as a pet.

TEMPERAMENT TESTS

In order to receive certain titles, a Fila Brasileiro is required to pass a temperament test. No other breed standard places as much importance on the temperament of the dog as that of the Fila Brasileiro. The Fila needs no training to pass the temperament test; in fact, it is a measure of his natural temperament, not something that is learned. The dog is required to go through several exercises that measure his behavior towards strangers, his reaction to visual and acoustic stimuli and his will-ingness to accompany the handler. He is also tested on his protective and aggressive behavior. A Fila is rated on his performance in these various tests. Any Fila that shows cowardice or aggression to his owner is immediately disquali-fied. These temperament tests are often performed at Fila Brasileiro specialty shows.

AGILITY TRIALS

Agility is designed so that the handler demonstrates how well the dog can work at his side. The handler directs his dog over an obstacle course that includes jumps as well as tires, the dog walk, weave poles, pipe tunnels, collapsed tunnels, etc. While working his way through the course, the dog must keep one eye and ear on the handler and the rest of his body on the course. The handler gives verbal and hand signals to guide the dog through the course.

The first organization to promote agility trials in the US was the United States Dog Agility Association, Inc. (USDAA), which was established in 1986 and spawned numerous member clubs around the country. The USDAA offers titles to winning dogs. Three titles are available through the USDAA: Agility Dog (AD), Advanced Agility Dog (AAD) and

Master Agility Dog (MAD). The American Kennel Club (AKC) offers similar titles at its trials: Novice Agility (NA), Open Agility (OA), Agility Excellent (AX) and Master Agility Excellent (MX). Beyond these four AKC titles, dogs can win additional ones in "jumper" classes, Jumpers with Weave Novice (NAJ), Open (OAJ) and Excellent (MXJ), which lead to the ultimate title(s): MACH, Master Agility Champion.

Agility is great fun for dog and owner with many rewards for everyone involved. Interested owners should join a training club that has obstacles and experi-enced agility handlers who can introduce you and your dog to the "ropes" (and tires, tunnels, etc.).

Best of Breed winner Leal do Camping, bred by Camping Kennel, owned by Mark and Kathy Koch and judged by Francisco Chapa Guajardo.

FILA BRASILEIRO

As a Fila Brasileiro owner, you have selected your dog so that you and your loved ones can have a companion, a protector, a friend and a four-legged family member. You invest time, money and effort to care for and train the family's new charge. Of course, this chosen canine behaves perfectly! Well, perfectly *like a dog*.

THINK LIKE A DOG

Dogs do not think like humans, nor do humans think like dogs, though we try. Unfortunately, a dog is incapable of figuring out how humans think, so the responsibility falls on the owner to adopt a proper canine mindset. Dogs cannot rationalize, and they exist in the present moment. Many a dog owner makes the mistake in training of thinking that he can reprimand his dog for something the dog did a while ago. You cannot even reprimand a dog for something he did 20 seconds ago! Either catch him in the act or forget it! It is a waste of your and your dog's time—in his mind, you are reprimanding him for whatever he is doing at that moment.

The following behavioral problems represent some which owners most commonly encounter. Every dog and every situation is unique. No author could purport for you to solve your Fila Brasileiro's problem simply by reading a chapter in a book. Here we outline some basic "dogspeak" so that owners' chances of solving behavioral problems are increased. Discuss bad habits with your veterinarian and he can recommend a behavioral specialist to consult in appropriate cases. Behavioral abnormalities are the leading reason that owners abandon their pets. Make a valiant effort to solve your Fila Brasileiro's problem. Patience and understanding are virtues that dwell in every pet-loving household.

AGGRESSION

This is the most obvious problem that concerns owners of the Fila Brasileiro. Aggression can be a very big problem in dogs, but more so with a powerful dog with a natural dislike of strangers. Aggression, when not controlled, always becomes dangerous. An aggressive dog may lunge at, bite or even attack a person or another dog. Aggressive behavior is not to be tolerated. It is more than just inappropriate behavior; it is not safe, especially with a tenacious, powerful breed like the Fila Brasileiro. It is painful for a family to watch their dog become unpredictable in his behavior to the point where they are afraid of him. It is important to ascertain why the dog is acting aggressively. Aggression is a display of dominance, and the dog should not have the dominant role in his pack.

It is important not to challenge an aggressive dog as this could provoke an attack. Observe your Fila Brasileiro's body language. Does he make direct eye contact and stare? Does he try to make himself as large as possible: ears alert, chest out, tail erect? Height and size signify authority in the dog pack—being taller or "above" another dog literally means that he is "above" in the social status. These body signals tell you that your Fila Brasileiro thinks he is in charge, a problem that needs to addressed.

The best solution is to consult a behavioral specialist, one who has experience with the Fila Brasileiro if possible. Together, perhaps you can pinpoint the cause of your dog's aggression and do something about it. An aggressive dog cannot be trusted, and a dog as powerful as the Fila that cannot be trusted is not safe to have as a family pet.

Filas are naturally protective and aggressive. Schutzhund or attack training for a dog as lethal as the Fila should be considered very carefully. Such training should only be undertaken by professionals in special situations.

AGGRESSION TOWARD OTHER DOGS
A dog's aggressive behavior toward another dog sometimes stems from insufficient exposure to other dogs at an early age. If other dogs make your Fila Brasileiro nervous and agitated, he will lash out as a defensive mechanism, though this behavior is thankfully uncommon in the breed. A dog who has not received sufficient exposure to other canines tends to believe that he is the only dog on the planet. The animal becomes so dominant that he does not even show signs that he is fearful or threatened. Without growling or any other physical signal as a warning, he will lunge at and bite the other dog. Although this is not a common problem, if you are concerned about your Fila's aggression towards other dogs, consult a behavioral specialist immediately.

DOMINANT AGGRESSION

A social hierarchy is firmly established in a wild dog pack. The dog wants to dominate those under him and please those above him. Dogs know that there must be a leader. If you are not the obvious choice for emperor, the dog will assume the throne! These conflicting innate desires are what a dog owner confronts when he sets about training a dog. In training a dog to obey commands, the owner is reinforcing that he is the top dog in the "pack" and that the dog should, and should want to, serve his superior. Thus, the owner is suppressing the dog's urge to dominate by modifying his behavior and making him obedient.

It is a constant effort to show the dog that his place in the pack is at the bottom. This is not meant to sound cruel or inhumane. You love your Fila Brasileiro and you should treat him with care and affection. Dog training is not about being cruel or feeling important, it is about molding the dog's behavior into what is acceptable and teaching him to live by your rules. In theory, it is quite simple: catch him in appropriate behavior and reward him for it. Add a dog into the equation and it becomes a bit more trying, but as a rule of thumb, positive reinforcement is what works best.

With a dominant dog, punishment and negative reinforcement

DINNER IS SERVED
An important part of training is taking every opportunity to reinforce that you are the leader. The simple action of making your Fila Brasileiro sit to wait for his food instead of allowing him to run up to get it when he wants it says that you control when he eats; he is dependent on you for food. Although it may be difficult, do not give in to your dog's wishes every time he whines at you or looks at you with pleading eyes.

can have the opposite effect of what you are after. It can make a dog fearful and/or act out aggressively if he feels he is being challenged. Remember, a dominant dog perceives himself at the top of the social heap and will fight to defend his perceived status. The best way to prevent that is never to give him reason to think that he is in control in the first place. If you are having trouble training your Fila Brasileiro and it seems as if he is constantly challenging your authority, seek the help of an obedience trainer or behavioral specialist. A professional will work with both you and your dog to teach you effective techniques to use at home. Beware of trainers who rely on excessively harsh methods; scolding is necessary now and then, but the focus in your training should always be on positive reinforcement.

If you can isolate what brings out the fear reaction, you can help the dog overcome it. Supervise your Fila Brasileiro's interactions with people and other dogs, and praise the dog when it goes well. If he starts to act aggressively in a situation, correct him and remove him from the situation. You are focusing on praise and on modifying his behavior by rewarding him when he acts appropriately. By being gentle and supervising his interactions, you are showing him that there is no need to be afraid or defensive.

SEXUAL BEHAVIOR

Dogs exhibit certain sexual behaviors that may have influenced your choice of male or female when you first purchased your Fila Brasileiro. To a certain extent, spaying/neutering will eliminate these behaviors, but if you are purchasing a dog that you wish to breed, you should be aware of what you will have to deal with throughout the dog's life.

Female dogs usually have two per year with each season lasting about three weeks. These are the only times in which a female dog will mate, and she usually will not allow this until the second week of the cycle. If a bitch is not bred during the heat cycle, it is not uncommon for her to experi-

This Fila is enjoying an afternoon snack. Keep harmful sticks and other objects away from your chewing Fila. These dogs can destroy practically anything they set their jaws to!

ence a false pregnancy, in which her mammary glands swell and she exhibits maternal tendencies toward toys or other objects.

Males tend to mark their territories, mount female dogs and other "friends" and may wander away from home in search of a bitch in heat. Owners must further recognize that mounting is not merely a sexual expression but also one of dominance.

CHEWING

The national canine pastime is chewing! Dogs need to chew, to massage their gums, to make their new teeth feel better and to exercise their jaws. This is a natural behavior deeply imbedded in all things canine. Your role as owner is not to stop the dog's chewing, but to redirect it to positive, chew-worthy objects. Be an informed owner and purchase proper chew toys like strong nylon bones that will not splinter. Be sure that the devices are safe and durable, since your dog's safety is at risk. Again, the owner is responsible for ensuring a dog-proof environment. The best answer is prevention: put your shoes, handbags and other tasty objects in their proper places (out of the reach of the growing canine mouth). Direct puppies to their toys whenever you see them tasting the furniture legs or the leg of your pants. Make a loud noise to attract the pup's attention and immediately escort him to his chew toy and engage him with the toy for at least four minutes, praising and encouraging him all the while.

Some trainers recommend deterrents, such as hot pepper or another bitter spice or a product designed for this purpose, to discourage the dog from chewing unwanted objects. Test out these products on your Fila before investing in a large quantity.

JUMPING UP
Jumping up is a dog's friendly way of saying hello! Some dog owners do not mind when their dog jumps up, which is fine for them. Your Fila is too large for such behavior and could harm a friend unintenionally. Given the breed's dislike of strangers, jumping up on unfamiliar visitors would rarely occur.

Pick a command such as "Off" (avoid using "Down" since you will use that for the dog to lie down) and tell him "Off" when he jumps up. Place him on the ground on all fours and have him sit, praising him the whole time. Always lavish him with praise and petting when he is in the sit position. That way you are still giving him a warm affectionate greeting, because you are as pleased to see him as he is to see you!

DIGGING
Digging, which is seen as a destructive behavior to humans, is actually quite a natural behavior in dogs. Although your Fila is not one of the "earth dogs" (also known as terriers), his desire to dig can be irrepressible and most frustrating to his owners. When digging occurs in your yard, it is actually a normal behavior redirected into something the dog can do in his everyday life. For example, in the wild a dog would be actively seeking food, making his own shelter, etc. He would be using his paws in a purposeful manner for his survival. Since you

understand what is permitted and what is not.

BARKING

Dogs cannot talk—oh, what they would say if they could! Instead, barking is a dog's way of "talking." It can be somewhat frustrating because it is not always easy to tell what a dog means by his bark—is he excited, happy, frightened or angry? Whatever it is that the dog is trying to say, he should not be punished for barking. It is only when the barking becomes excessive and a bad habit, does the behavior need to be modified.

If an intruder came into your home in the middle of the night and the dog barked a warning, wouldn't you be pleased? You would probably deem your dog a hero, a wonderful guardian and protector of the home. On the other hand, if a friend drops by unexpectedly and rings the doorbell and is greeted with a sudden sharp bark, you would probably be annoyed at the dog. But isn't it just the same behavior? The dog does not know any better...unless he sees who is at the door and it is someone he knows, he will bark as a means of vocalizing that his (and your) territory is being threatened. While your friend is not posing a threat, it is all the same to the dog. Barking is his means of letting you know that there is an intrusion, whether friend or foe, on your property.

HE'S PROTECTING YOU

Barking is your dog's way of protecting you. If he barks at a stranger walking past your house, a moving car or a fleeing cat, he is merely exercising his responsibility to protect his pack *(you)* and territory from a perceived intruder. Since the "intruder" usually keeps going, the dog thinks his barking chased it away and he feels fulfilled. This behavior leads your overly vocal friend to believe that he is the "dog in charge."

provide him with food and shelter, he has no need to use his paws for these purposes, and so the energy that he would be using manifests itself in the form of little holes all over your yard and flower beds.

Of course, digging is easiest to control if it is stopped as soon as possible, but it is often hard to catch a dog in the act, especially if he is alone in the yard during the day. If your dog is a compulsive digger and not easily distracted by other activities, you can designate an area on your property where it is okay for him to dig. If you catch him digging in an off-limits area of the yard, immediately lead him to the approved area and praise him for digging there. Keep a close eye on him so that you can catch him, that is the only way he is going to

This type of barking is instinctive and should not be discouraged.

Excessive habitual barking is a problem that should be corrected early on. As your Fila Brasileiro grows up, you will be able to tell when his barking is purposeful and when it is for no reason. You will become able to distinguish your dog's different barks and their meanings. For example, the bark when someone comes to the door will be different from the bark when he is excited to see you. It is similar to a person's tone of voice, except that the dog has to rely totally on tone of voice because he does not have the benefit of using words. An incessant barker will be evident at an early age.

There are some things that encourage a dog to bark. For example, if your dog barks non-stop for a few minutes and you give him a treat to quiet him, he believes that you are rewarding him for barking. He will associate barking with getting a treat, and will keep doing it until he is rewarded.

FOOD STEALING
Is your dog devising ways of stealing food from your coffee table? If so, you must answer the following questions: Is your Fila hungry, or is he "constantly famished" like many dogs seem to be? Face it, some dogs are more food-motivated than others.

Some dogs are totally obsessed by the smell of food and can only think of their next meal. Food stealing is terrific fun and always yields a great reward—*food*, glorious food.

The owner's goal, therefore, is to be sensible about where food is placed in the home, and to reprimand your dog whenever caught in the act of stealing. But remember, only reprimand the dog if you actually see him stealing, not later when the crime is discovered for that will be of no use at all and will only serve to confuse.

BEGGING
Just like food stealing, begging is a favorite pastime of hungry puppies! It yields that same super reward—*food!* Dogs quickly learn that their owners keep the "good food" for ourselves, and that we humans do not dine on dry food alone. Begging is a conditioned response related to a specific stimulus, time and place. The sounds of the kitchen, cans and bottles opening, crinkling bags, the smell of food in preparation, and the like will excite the dog and soon the nose is in the air!

Here is the solution to stopping this behavior: Never give in to a beggar! You are rewarding the dog for sitting pretty, whining and rubbing his nose into you by giving him that glorious reward—*food*. By ignoring the dog, you

"X" MARKS THE SPOT

As a pack animal, your dog marks his territory as a way of letting any possible intruders know that this is his space and that he will defend his territory if necessary. Your dog marks by urinating because urine contains pheromones that allow other canines to identify him. While this behavior seems like a nuisance, it speaks volumes about your dog's mental health. Stable, well-trained dogs living in quiet, less populated areas may mark less frequently than less confident dogs inhabiting busy urban areas that attract many possible invaders. If your dog only marks in certain areas in your home, your bed or just the front door, these are the areas he feels obligated to defend. If your dog marks frequently, see your veterinarian or an animal behaviorist.

will (eventually) force the behavior into extinction. Note that the behavior likely gets worse before it disappears, so be sure there are not any "softies" in the family who will give in to little "Oliver" every time he whimpers, "More, please."

SEPARATION ANXIETY

Your Fila may howl, whine or otherwise vocalize his displeasure at your leaving the house and his being left alone. This is a normal reaction, no different than the child who cries as his mother leaves him on the first day at school. In fact, constant attention can lead to separation anxiety in the first place. If you are endlessly fussing over your dog, he will come to expect this from you all of the time and it will be more traumatic for him when you are not there. Obviously, you enjoy spending time with your dog, and he thrives on your love and attention. However, it should not become a dependent relationship in which he is heartbroken without you.

One thing you can do to minimize separation anxiety is to make your entrances and exits as low-key as possible. Do not give your dog a long drawn-out goodbye, and do not lavish him with hugs and kisses when you return. This is giving him the attention that he craves, and it will only make him miss it more when you are away. When the dog is alone in the house, he should be confined to his designated dog-proof area of the house. This should be the area in which he sleeps and already feels comfortable so he will feel more at ease when he is alone. Another thing you can try is to give your dog a treat when you leave; this will not only keep him occupied and keep his mind off the fact that you just left, but it will also help him associate your leaving with a pleasant experience.

INDEX

Page numbers in **boldface** indicate illustrations.

My Fila Brasileiro

PUT YOUR PUPPY'S FIRST PICTURE HERE

Dog's Name _____

Date _____ Photographer _____